Freud's Student Years

In *Freud's Student Years*, Florian Houssier presents the life experiences and inner conflicts of Sigmund Freud from his eighteenth birthday to his clinical practice, showing how these experiences informed his later theories.

Following on from *Freud's Adolescence: Oedipus Complex and Parricidal Tendencies* (2023) and starting at the point of the young Freud's graduation, Houssier charts the inception of Freud's ideas on fantasy, the Madonna-Whore complex, the Oedipal Complex, mother-daughter relationships and narcissism. Working chronologically, he looks at the way Freud's reflection and lamentation on his inhibited adolescence led to a fantasy of possession that informed his later work. Including excerpts from Freud's private letters to his fiancée, Martha Bernays, and exploring his relationship with Sándor Ferenczi, this volume offers a unique and intimate look into the life and inner workings of the most eminent figure of modern psychoanalysis.

Accessible in style and thorough in its assessments of Freud's personal experiences, this book is an essential read for psychoanalysts and psychologists, as well as students and scholars interested in the history of psychoanalysis and the enduring legacy of Freudian thought.

Florian Houssier is a clinical psychologist and psychoanalyst (Société de Psychanalyse Freudienne). He is Professor of Clinical Psychology and Psychopathology at the Sorbonne, France; Director of the Laboratory Transversal Unit of Research: Psychogenesis and Psychopathology (UTRPP); and President of the Collège International de L'Adolescence (CILA).

Freud's Student Years

A Psychobiography

Florian Houssier

Routledge
Taylor & Francis Group

LONDON AND NEW YORK

Cover image: GeorgiosArt/© Getty Images

First published by Campagne-Première in Paris as Freud étudiant,
24 avril 2019. ISBN 9782372060486

The translation is based on the French edition of the book: Freud
étudiant
By Florian Houssier

Campagne-Première © 2019
ISBN 9782372060486

First published in English 2025
by Routledge
4 Park Square, Milton Park, Abingdon, Oxon OX14 4RN

and by Routledge
605 Third Avenue, New York, NY 10158

*Routledge is an imprint of the Taylor & Francis Group, an informa
business*

©2025 Florian Houssier

British Library Cataloguing-in-Publication Data
A catalogue record for this book is available from the British
Library

ISBN: 978-1-032-56769-3 (hbk)
ISBN: 978-1-032-56768-6 (pbk)
ISBN: 978-1-003-43706-2 (ebk)

DOI: 10.4324/9781003437062

Typeset in Times New Roman
by Apex CoVantage, LLC

Contents

Introduction

We left young Sigmund just as he had passed his baccalaureate (Houssier, 2018a). What remained of his adolescent experience? What traces did it leave behind? What kept adolescence alive for the young monk Philemon with whom Freud identified in Charles Kingsley's novel? Did the story of a monk tormented by his incestuous desire remain significant in young Freud's psychic life?

As we pick up the thread of his journey, several strains of associations emerge, sketching out a portrait I will try and restore. Freud's romantic and sexual life was reduced to its simplest expressions, which, as his letters to his fiancée later confirmed, was a source of great suffering for the inhibited young man. However, if we think of sexuality beyond its physical aspects, we glimpse a series of fantasies, e.g., Freud's occasional fascination with the mother-daughter relationship (Houssier, 2017a). We remember his encounter with Gisela Fluss' mother Eleanora, which implicitly made him rediscover the love for his own mother. The displacement of his desire towards Gisela's mother created a tension: she was both the object of repression – he couldn't remember her coming into his room at night – and of desire. She was idealised as the perfect mother, raising her children while remaining modern and sophisticated. Incestuous sexuality versus culture – this theme indeed runs throughout Freud's entire body of work.

In addition to the projection of his own narcissism, Eleonora was also the ideal equivalent of his own mother Amalia, who was thus implicitly criticised – so much so that Freud nearly forgot Gisela, his "official" love object when writing to Eduard Silberstein. We also discussed the function of Freud's infatuation with Gisela in his psychic life; she represented both an internal object, melancholised by the absence of any but a fantasy relationship. At the same time, she served as a pretext, mediating his sublimated homosexual love for Eduard and thus propping up both heterosexual masculinity and bisexuality. Gisela also embodied the part of the lost pre-Oedipal object, fuelling his feelings of sadness and depression as a young boy. This series of representations, which is most likely incomplete, includes another matrix of fantasies. We have seen two situations in which Freud was fascinated by mother-daughter duos: Gisela and her mother, but also the incident on the train, where he was captivated by a pre-pubescent girl resembling a young page, accompanied by her mother. In the following pages, we will find two more examples

DOI: 10.4324/9781003437062-1

of this attraction, this time featuring Eduard and later Martha, to corroborate the hypothesis that we can only explore the libidinal figures of Gisela and Eleanora by seeing them as undoubtedly linked together, rather than separate. These dyads offer another perspective, which I will discuss at the end of the book – the idea of representing highly charged objects as doubles. This also has to do with Freud's search for his own double, which also started during his adolescent years.

At the same time, we should keep in mind that already during this period, Freud's place as the firstborn son came closely to that of the *pater familias*. His parents asked him to choose the name for his youngest brother: Freud named him after one of his literary heroes, Alexander the Great. The same brother later appeared in the events described in Freud's 1936 paper *The Disturbance of Memory on the Acropolis*, a text which can be seen as a key moment of theorising Freud's own adolescence. It is nevertheless the case that as he began his university studies, Freud's parents nurtured his fantasies of omnipotence in the family, as a firstborn son with a brilliant future, intellectually superior but strictly repressing any potential encounter with the other sex.

There is no doubt that the intense struggle against his sexual fantasies which Freud waged during this time contributed to the traumatic and sexually repressed nature of his adolescence (Houssier, Gutton, 2018): the paralysing inhibition experienced with Gisela was connected to the fulfilment of grandiose, incestuous and heroic fantasies. His later long-distance relationship with his fiancée Martha Bernays also included a fantasy of possession – she belonged to him – underpinned by a regret of not having properly benefited sexually from his youth.

Freud's often acute suffering during this time was due not just to his inhibitions but also to the pressures of poverty. His entire later part of adolescence, if we consider it as such, was marked by the weight of his parents' legacy: his father Jacob's professional failure and his mother's Oedipal promise, where his mother's nickname for him, "the Golden Sigi", transformed into a project of becoming a great man. Both Jacob and Amalia entrusted their son with the generational mandate of repairing their struggling family. The narcissistic wound of his father's bankruptcy combined with the constant difficulties of finding money to support his family, which accentuated and indefinitely prolonged Freud's conflicts and ambivalence towards his father and towards other men close to him, as later seen in the paradigmatic case of Ferenczi.

For now, during the summer of 1873, the summer before he entered the Faculty of Medicine, we find Freud was learning French and philosophy with his friend Braun, while Eduard was getting ready to leave Vienna to study in Germany. Freud was still living in his literary world; the written word was over-invested, while we see a distancing from potential love objects, as a kind of effort to create a containing envelope that could tolerate the unbearable nature of certain pubertal ideas. The unconscious choice of Cervantes' novella, *The Dialogue of the Dogs*, which became a reference shared with Eduard to create an intimate language of their friendship, is highly significant as a story about witches conveying the horror of incest. This rejection, fairly typical of adolescence, went hand in hand with a line of flight that for young Freud always led through literature and the arts. However, what we see is not just a phobic tendency but also an effort to contain his conflicts in order to sublimate them better. Is this a kind of denial of his pubertal sensoriality (Houssier, Gutton, 2018), which provokes unbearable representations that must quickly be transformed into ideas or even theory? The following pages will try to shed some light on these questions. They show a fundamental transformation, the slow disinvesting of the relationship with his closest friend at this time, in favour of an academic and professional trajectory marked by a search for mostly male figures of identification. While not always following a strictly chronological narrative, we will focus on four thematic groups, also considering, despite the fragmentary nature of the material,[1] another central aspect of Freud's adolescence: his encounter with his future wife, Martha. I have already pointed out (Houssier, 2018a) that this most important love relationship of Freud's life was a continuation of the still ongoing adolescent process. Hence the importance of identifying the key examples of the retroactive effects of his adolescence, which highlight its legacy in Freud's psychic life.

Let us now go back to Freud's letters to Eduard and his fiancée, and again try to think about young Freud's trajectory, full of pitfalls but also creativity.

Note

1 The five volumes of Freud's courtship letters have so far only been published in German, which I did not have access to. My discussion is thus based on those letters that have been translated into French and a number of articles on the matter.

Chapter 1

Student life

According to Breger (2000) it was only at the age of nineteen, when the Freuds moved into a larger flat, that Sigmund finally had his own room, his "cabinet". Here he would sleep and keep his growing collection of books, fleeing his mother and sisters into his own world.

The period of his medical studies appears as a kind of teenage moratorium, to use Erikson's expression (1950): a time when a young person gradually becomes a student, looking for his own way in life and building a sense of identity. During this time, Freud's various projects proliferated, essentially tending towards the humanities. His mind was occupied by poetry, philosophy, politics, but also psychology, while his desire to finish his medical degree and find a university post remained constant, though not without a degree of conflict. His initial wish to study for a double degree was made difficult by his medical studies but compensated for by various encounters and reading. Joining a physiology laboratory as an assistant spelled the beginning of a promising and versatile career.

1.1 To love and to work

1.1.1 A passion for the humanities

Looking back over his life, Freud (1925) said that on starting university, he was made familiar with the situation of being in the opposition and under the ban of the "compact majority", which gave him the foundations for an independence of judgment. His "youthful eagerness" pushed him towards scientific topics for which he lacked talent. Quoting Goethe's *Faust*, he described his disappointment: "'It is in vain that you range around from science to science: each man learns only what he can learn'" (Goethe, *Faust*, Part I, Scene 4, quoted in Freud, 1925, p. 9).

In the autumn of 1873, he enrolled at the Vienna University; he graduated in March 1881, at a time when his relationship with Eduard Silberstein was ending. This three-year "delay" in completing his medical degree might seem surprising in such a gifted student. As Freud himself explained, "another thing prevents me from studying: a tendency to devote myself to research, which makes me sacrifice many things, the dissatisfaction with what students are offered, the need to get into the

DOI: 10.4324/9781003437062-2

details and be critical" (Eissler, 2006, p. 12, translated). For Eissler, this fondness for research meant that Freud was a scientist rather than a student. The long period of studies finally ended after Freud passed three oral examinations (the so-called *rigorosa*), while simultaneously working at the Institute of Physiology. His first piece of research was linked to his zoology professor, Carl Claus. He was granted two scholarships by the Ministry of Education, to study male freshwater eels at the Centre for Zoology in Trieste, which resulted in his first publication (Freud, 1877). Carl Brühl's lectures also shifted his interest towards histology and science (Eissler, 1978). Apparently disappointed by his research, he then decided to join Professor Brücke's physiology laboratory, where he worked from 1876 until 1882.

Although he was tempted by the humanities, Freud remained faithful to his intention of studying medicine. In a letter to Eduard, he at first expressed his wish to spend his university years on "purely humanistic studies" (Freud, 1871–1881, p. 24) at the philosophy faculty, which would be unrelated to medicine but, he believed, useful. He then suggested his friend joined him to make "your first cut on a human cadaver in my company". In a later letter to his fiancée, he spoke about another friend, Robert Franceschini, with whom he began his medical studies. There were three of them in his class to choose medicine, and they all scribbled their names on a jointly bought skeleton (Freud, 1873–1939, p. 42).

For now, having obtained his baccalaureate, his position remained mixed: he did not yet want to choose a career and simply wished to be seen as educated and knowledgeable, perhaps becoming a professor. He confided in Eduard that he did not want his mother to find out about the epidemy of cholera in Vienna, in order not to worry her unnecessarily in case the rumours were exaggerated. The letter ended with another demand that Eduard kept his letters secret, so that he could write frankly and about anything that came to his mind. The project was still latent, but especially since Freud read Börne's work, a way of thinking began to impose itself as a free and associative counterpart to his otherwise increasing rigidity around sensual conflicts.

His position towards girls changed, though very slightly. He confided in Eduard his longing for the "angelic glances" he previously "confessed to" and which he could not find "at home", but elsewhere, where they were lacking: "I yearn for them because I do not possess them." He was surprised when his friend misunderstood his joke, reading the word play on "angelic" and "English glance" as a wish to be seen angelically by the girls in the house, rather than young ladies outside. But at home, there were none, Freud explained (1873–1939, p. 41). This misunderstanding could also be read as Eduard's unintended interpretation, suggesting that unconsciously Freud still expected far too much from his family to receive any attention from girls.

As for Eduard, after his Matura he moved to Leipzig for a year to study law, focusing on the history of political and social sciences and on socio-democratic ideas. This new separation, which for the first time extended beyond the period of the school holidays, had initially little effect on the tone of their letters. Freud wrote that it was not out of despair that he had chosen to explore philosophy and that for the moment, he had become an anglophile, a vice that might threaten his salvation. He immersed himself in English poetry, history and literature.

Trying to reach his ideal, to become a great man and surpass his elders by a victory challenging past achievements – this was Freud's plan and the path he diligently followed. His daydreams of glory helped him articulate his career ambitions and simultaneously attenuated his daily struggles, at a time when he was still largely hesitating as to which path to take to make his fantasies a reality.

1.1.2   A world falling apart

Having started his practical training in anatomy and physiology, Freud also began to attend the lectures of the philosopher Brentano, while Eduard followed those of Fechner. He outlined his schedule as including fifty-one and a half hours of lectures per week, plus an hour of swimming and additional reading. He confided in Eduard as to a confessor able to keep his secrets – or to a future psychoanalyst. He described his semi-nocturnal way of life, studying from ten to two o'clock at night, but "quite often over-stretching my energies until four or five". This nocturnal greediness was of course not without effect: he would then feel unable to study for a day or two, "lost" a period of time, preferring to live in accordance with the phases of the moon. His course of study was "fairly large scale" (1873–1939, p. 87), including all the natural sciences and astronomy, in addition to anatomy, physiology, zoology, physics and mathematics, as well as Darwinism and, of course, the biological and organic sciences in the following years. This amount of activity prevented him from reading as many novels as before – he restricted himself to "a little Lessing or Goethe" or Lichtenberg. He nevertheless still had time to reread a chapter of *Don Quixote*, "and experience an idyllic moment". At six o'clock in the morning, alone in his room with something to eat, he read the scene in which Pedro Recio de Tirtaefuera[1] took away from poor Sancho everything he wanted to taste. In the following letter, Freud's lifestyle appeared to be more conflictual; he apologised for the delay in answering Eduard's letter, leading to a self-reproach, of feeling overwhelmed without really having studied a great deal. He had gone in too many directions. He was sleeping only four hours a day, feeling impatient, like someone "expecting this world to end within a fortnight and whom a professor's chair awaits in the next" (Ibid., p. 89).

1.1.3   The challenge of loss

After having advised his friend, who was about to embark on a career in law, to choose a university in Germany or Switzerland, Freud's letter adopted a more passionate tone, when he complained about the absence of Spanish from their recent correspondence. He lamented: "For how long will one still be able to speak of an *aetas aurea*[2] of the Spanish Academy?" (Ibid. p. 55). This kind of nostalgia was part of the experience of losing an idealised relationship; on the other hand, its golden age reminds us of the "golden Sigi" and another kind of glorious past – of being his mother's little treasure.

The reaction to these feelings of loss was not long in coming. Freud put up a fierce struggle to maintain the relationship. The following letter again called for the resuscitation of the Spanish Academy; he suggested the project was exciting because of the distance between them. He described himself as a modern man with twelve-hour working days, in a "whirl of duties and tasks" (Ibid., p. 57) and dreamless nights. Given both of their tight schedules, he argued that in order for their friendship to work, each of them would have to commit to a task, which would be the only thing "to make our separation tolerable" (Ibid.) and demanded this task to be fulfilled "at fixed times and with unswerving devotion". In the context of their studies and busy lives, the solution was to write to each other every Sunday, a long letter that would be "nothing short of an entire encyclopaedia of the past week", with "total veracity reports all our doings". These documents would constitute the Academy's archives, with the aim of discovering "enough of interest within us". He felt the need not to become a doctor or an out-and-out bohemian, by staying informed about what was happening at other universities and in other disciplines. He wanted to "preserve some spirit of romantism" of the Academy; to turn each letter into an issue of a weekly journal. At the end of the letter, he nonetheless took the opposite stance: it should not be a school homework but a chance to work freely, "an informal piece and a communication" (Ibid., p. 58) based on each person's introspection.

Another theme returned to illustrate the dreams of seeing Eduard again, that of an intimate stroll: "I suspect walks, unconscious searching, and undesired yet hotly desired discovery" (Ibid., p. 89), with a memory of a rose-garden, a feast of dahlias, so that it is difficult to say whether Freud was talking about strolling with a girl, Eduard or both. If we connect some of these elements, we see that Freud's teenage years were a crucible for his future psychoanalytic career. Finding things of interest in oneself was part of the same investigation as "unconscious searching", also driven by a longing for the hotly desired libidinised relations.

In this letter, Freud informed Eduard that he had taken some photographs of himself and had set one aside for him, with a little poem on the back. This "effigy" would cost Eduard his own head in return – Freud's way of again asking for not one but two pictures of him, one for himself and the other for the family album. He returned to the question in the following letter, threatening to demand his sisters to ask Eduard for a picture; the expression "foisting them onto the principles" also suggests that the "principles" could include his sisters.

After a year apart, except for a brief meeting, in September 1875 Freud again wanted to rekindle the Academy's flame, hoping to meet his friend in Vienna in the following year. During the winter, Eduard was to leave Leipzig and return to Vienna. He re-enrolled at the Faculty of Law – he received his degree in 1879 – and in turn became interested in Brentano's teaching, to which I will return in more detail.

Imagining the shared walks and discussions, Freud wrote: "We shall be able to exchange words for words and, God willing, thoughts for thoughts as well: I really believe that we shall never be rid of each other" (Ibid., p. 126). The sentence is significant in terms of a possible displacement: the language of the body that belonged to the forest walks with his father, hand in hand, or again arm in arm with Eduard (Houssier, 2017b), was now replaced by the sharing of thoughts, fuelling the fantasy of an unbreakable bond, where each of them would communicate directly with the other's mind. The struggle against loss and for the maintenance of an idealised object was at its most intense.

1.1.4   A friend is a complement

Having chased away these fears, Freud asked Eduard to suggest what book he would like for his birthday, explaining that he had a "free hand" at the university bookstore, already making the fullest use of. In his letter of 11th December 1874, an amicable conflict broke out around the topic of the birthday present: it seems that Eduard rejected a gift sent by Freud, one of the rules of the Academy in fact prohibiting birthday presents. Freud protested, pointing out that it was Eduard who had first broken the rule and if the rule no longer fitted, it should be changed. He gave Eduard an ultimatum: either he told him which book he would like, or he ran the risk of receiving an anonymous one, without a dedication.

In the following letter, the dispute continued; Freud felt misunderstood and took on a more serious, less humourous stance. The rule against birthday gifts seemed obsolete. On a more playful note, he wrote that if Eduard thought he could defer until the next birthday, Freud would be forced to dispatch the book "by illegal means" (Freud, 1873–1939, p. 79). In the following letter, Freud suggested gifting him his *Don Quixote*, in the spirit of the Academy. He could also give him a book by Ernst Haeckel, a professor of zoology at Iéna and a follower of Darwin, who formulated the fundamental biogenetic law.

He complained of Eduard's postcards, which deprived him of more substantial letters, and predicted that one day, letters will be replaced by telegrams, so that one would be able to correspond with a friend for a decade without ever seeing their handwriting. In the end, he proposed giving Eduard his own copy of *Don Quixote*, explaining that the only book worth gifting was one perused by a friend, which he or she relinquished in order to please the other. Otherwise, the gift remained an insignificant object anyone could buy. He was rather preoccupied with the question of exchanging gifts, so much so that he thought it should be regulated by a law. By saying that the opposite party was only waiting to reciprocate one's present as quickly as possible, he designated the other as an adversary (Ibid., p. 81). There was no question of trying to be quits through well-established social conventions; he instead suggested the matter be "decided by casting lots, to obviate that scrupulous regularity and punctuality which is the enemy of all surprises" (Ibid.).

Freud also said the two of them preferred to show their friendship through actions rather than words; merely calling the other "dear friend" made him blush in embarrassment. And yet at the time, nothing gave him more satisfaction than these warm and friendly words. Despite this hyper-sensibility, the blushing that betrayed the (homo)sexual nature of his feelings, whether conscious or not, he recognised the importance of feeling cared for and supported. This moment of speaking freely about their friendship was an opportunity to express just how painful their long separation was, and that a letter would make up for the absence. Finally, he added, with great sincerity: "The gap your absence has opened in my social life has remained unfilled, nor have I ever looked for anyone to fill it" (Ibid., 77). He was not interested in having many friends, but he cared about the quality of the friendship; he had formed a more cordial relationship with Wahle (Houssier, 2018a), whose naïve idealism he found endearing. He also spoke about Paneth and their lively intellectual discussions; but while Paneth was amiable, Freud found him too self-absorbed. However, the deeper reason was that Paneth would hardly think to "seek his complement in a friend" (1873–1939, p. 77). The narcissistic dimension of this search for a double as an alter ego in order to create a supportive and secure relational space is close to what some authors have commented on as the twin-like bond between the two friends (Ibid.) This idea of searching for a friend as a complement also "prepared" the later encounter with Fliess, giving friendship a distinctly narcissistic flavour.

On 31st December 1874, Freud was thinking of his friend: this was the first time they were not spending Christmas and New Year's Eve together. With Eduard, Freud felt "saved" from his solitude. Eduard took on the tasks he himself felt unfit to do, such as entertaining the "youthful company" that gathered to celebrate his sister Anna's sixteenth birthday. We notice another sign of his depressive tendencies: feeling alone when surrounded by others. As we have already seen, the youthful company was essentially feminine. The account of his feelings was also permeated by sadness: growing up was a sad process. Freud alluded to something having changed between them – they were no longer schoolboys hoping to see each other during the winter holidays. Each now had to abide by the contingencies of their respective choices and paths, which separated them, without any guarantee of finding each other again.

1.1.5 The gold of books: the position of the father

In the letter dated 11th December 1874, Freud portrayed himself as a not particularly diligent student, but with a pleasant prospect: each month to enlarge his "beloved small library, which gives me infinite pleasure" (Ibid., p. 78). He continued: "As for the source of my funds, you know very well that the firm of W. Braumüller, the largest bookstore in Vienna, is at my unlimited disposal." The signifiers "funds", "largest" and "unlimited" come together with all their associative resonances: the Golden Sigi was happy to grow up and become a great man with unlimited ambition, especially in the cultural and literary fields.

Two episodes from his teenage years suggest that the infantile may sometime function as a screen against the pubertal; the former, which we have already explored, shows the temporal reversibility of the screen memory (Freud, 1899). Not only does the memory of his youth function as a screen against infantile sexual wishes, but the opposite is true as well. Freud confirms this in his comments on the dream of the botanical monograph and his passion for reading:

> I had always, from the time I first began to think about myself, referred this first passion of mine back to the childhood memory I have mentioned. Or rather, I had recognized that the childhood scene was a 'screen memory' for my later bibliophile propensities. And I had early discovered, of course, that passions often lead to sorrow.
>
> (Freud, 1900, pp. 172–173)

We have seen that Freud's passion for books originated in the memory of tearing out, together with his sister Anna, the pages of a book on a journey through Persia, but also that this memory functioned as a screen against another memory of his youth (Houssier, 2015b). The French word for what Freud and his sister were doing, *effeuillage* – "stripping" – makes the erotic nature of the memory even clearer, giving it a high libidinal charge. As if continuing an inner dialogue with a paternal figure, Freud (1900) returns to this autobiographical sequence when he remembers that as a young boy, he ran up a debt with his favourite bookseller, provoking an angry reaction from his father, while Freud himself considered his passion for books a relatively suitable outlet for his inclinations. He writes:

> When I was seventeen I had run up a largish account at the bookseller's and had nothing to meet it with; and my father had scarcely taken it as an excuse that my inclinations might have chosen a worse outlet. The recollection of this experience from the later years of my youth at once brought back to my mind the conversation with my friend Dr. Königstein. For in the course of it we had discussed the same question of my being blamed for being too much absorbed in my favourite hobbies.
>
> (Freud, 1900, p. 173)

His comments conceal a castration fantasy. His father could have thought that the company of books was preferable to that of girls, or indeed to masturbation, but he did not take his son's wisdom into account and criticised his debts, which, on writing his book on dreams, Freud seems to regret. Faced with the onslaught of genital sexuality, his solution to his "inclinations", both a phobic mechanism and a form of sublimation, was allegedly criticised by his father, leaving a degree of resentment. The idea of being too absorbed in his hobbies could be understood as a sign of a struggle against masturbatory fantasies, which were likely fuelled by his extensive reading and philosophical reveries.

In addition, he comments on his student-day passion for books in his analysis of the same dream. His desire to collect and accumulate books, to become a "bookworm", attests to his use of highly erotised intellectual activity as a defence against sexual fantasies.

An associative link connects Freud's favourite flower, the cyclamen, with his favourite food, the artichoke, also a plant, and with the bookworm, which of course prefers to feast on books. In this association, pulling out the leaves of a (beautiful) flower highlights the sexualisation of his memories, in which his sister Anna was, like his cousin Pauline, an object of attention in a shared scene witnessed by an adult, who comes to the rescue or gives permission. He continues his analysis by referring to Fliess:

> I had had a letter from my friend in Berlin the day before in which he had shown his power of visualization: "I am very much occupied with your dream-book. I see it lying finished before me and I see myself turning over its pages." How much I envied him his gift as a seer! If only I could have seen it lying finished before me!
>
> (Freud, 1900, p. 172)

1.1.6   The beginnings of a first journal

The Spanish Academy was the first learned society Freud founded, before the Wednesday Psychological Society and the organisations that followed, but also before the unceasing work of writing, both scientific and personal. Although it has disappeared without a trace, possibly in his first auto-da-fé, we also know that Freud kept a journal. To this first tool of internal self-dialogue, we can also add his wish to create the archives of the Spanish Academy, as a kind of logbook of their friendship.

But the comparison goes further; in 1875, Freud also created the first journal with his university friends. Two issues were published, before he announced the journal had come to an end. This was part of his larger interest in the human psyche and relationships, but with one important difference, namely that a journal was a point of contact with the outside world, contrary to the intimate universe only shared with Eduard. Freud did not go through this process of opening up alone, but together with his peers.

After a first unsuccessful attempt, Freud wrote to Eduard that he had founded a new journal, this time together with Lipiner, Paneth and Lowy. He informed him that a second issue had already been published, but also that a new fraternity, "Austria", had been formed. He named the shared acquaintances involved – Schmeidel, Fleischer, Löwy, Conrad, Müller and Baiersdorf – but explained that he had not been invited to join, and would hope that Eduard too would therefore stay away. He justified this in the following letter: students could sometimes be arrogant and instead of studying spent their time on drinking, gossiping and political drivel (Freud, 1873–1939, p. 78). He asked Eduard to stay free from such fraternising, like "an honest Fink", i.e., a student free of associations. At the time, most of

German-speaking students were members of different groups, often distinguishing themselves by wearing caps of different colours.

On a lighter note, Freud announced the early death of this second journal, saying that after he had given it life and seen it suffer, he also delivered the death blow; he must now keep his philosophical thinking to himself or pass it unrefined to Paneth.

As if in a couple threatened by monotony and indifference, Freud stuck to his line with Eduard, passionate and fiery, in stark contrast to the desire for openness manifested by the founding of a scientific journal. Later when their friendship began to fade, he wrote regarding the productions of the Spanish Academy: "I invite you to conjure up a nice winter evening when together we shall burn the archives in a solemn auto-da-fé" (p. 167), an invitation resembling the creation of a rite of passage. For the first time, we see what later became Freud's constant preoccupation: not leaving any traces, making this destruction a quasi-sacred moment, worthy of the "great man" he was convinced to become one day. He wanted to share this adolescent ritual and its symbolic importance with his friend, seeing it as a kind of self-proclaimed mourning for his youth, tending towards the idea of growing up. Nostalgically, he also lamented the loss of "the original purity of Spanish manners and customs", which had become blemished, finally adding, as if in anticipation of what he would later write to Martha about his biographers, but in a rather humoristic tone: "I shudder at the work of the historiographers and cultural historians who will have to paint the picture of this sad decline" (p. 55).

1.1.7   Going to Berlin

Speaking about his plans to attend the lectures of Dubois-Reymond, Helmholtz or Virchow in Berlin during the winter semester of 1875–1876, Freud explained that, if money could be found, his father was already in agreement. For once, he was the one to initiate a separation in favour of the "advantageous" idea of seeing the world "in some of its most godforsaken places" (Freud, 1871–1881, p. 84). Freud dreamt of travel – he wanted to see the world out there; its imagined beauty and encounters with prominent people resonated with the intensity of his ambitions.

In the following letter, he again asked his friend for a photograph, fuelling the hopes of seeing him in Berlin for a semester or two: "Then we should have achieved the ideal, idyllic state of the A.E. we envisaged two years ago on our Styrian tour" (Ibid., p 86). In this "shared novel", Freud had the idea of living with Eduard rather than Braun, who also wanted to come to Berlin. He preferred the simplicity and the Arcadian poetry of the Spanish Academy, taking his friend's moderation and thrift as his model, unless, he said, Eduard had renounced them in the meantime, as his last letter suggested. "You would have to dig them out again for my sake", Freud added, then went on to describe his daily schedule: lectures, laboratories, studying, "but the evenings should be ours", as well as one day in the week. On this topic, he thought they could resume their old study tours or "secret walks, perhaps with principles" – a "perhaps" that speaks volumes about the intensity of Freud's friendly feelings, while leaving open the new possibility of a third person between them. This gesture was a sign of a "secondarisation" of their relationship, as a more nuanced link. Indeed, its passionate aspect was fading; however, this was later counteracted by Freud's jealousy, disguised as his strict moral stance vis-à-vis the "principles". In this exchange, the idealised yet not unrealistic plan so dear to Freud was to live with his friend *and* be fully committed to his studies, to "have it all" in Berlin, far from the family troubles. He added that while Roznau was "the first promised land of our friendship" and Styria the second, Berlin could well be the third. Travel would gradually free him from his primary family bonds: Roznau was linked to both his mother and Freiberg, and Styria represented the first journey, at a time when their friendship could only exist in the family context. Berlin established a distance from his family but also created a shared student life. Once again, the intention to live in Berlin and the idea of living with a friend repeated in the case of Freud's daughter Anna. In 1919, she wrote to her brother Ernst (Freud, A., 1919) that she wished to go live in Berlin and create a psychoanalytic publishing house there. Shortly after, Freud's announcement that he was suffering from the cancer of the jaw (Schavelzon, 1983) put an end to Anna's desire for independence. While remaining a "vestal", she later found a compromise, living in Vienna and later in London with her partner Dorothy Burlingham (Houssier, 2010).

Nevertheless, Freud's Berlin plan failed for no apparent reason, and later took on a new and less exciting direction. There seems to have been another possibility of living with his friend, equally tentative and unrealised, which Freud mentioned in his letter of 2nd October 1875. His father arranged for Eduard and his brother to stay with a family friend from Freiberg, using a ruse to convince Eduard to accept his offer. The brief description suggests this was a joint plan between Freud and his father. Freud only regretted that the accommodation was too far from the university. On the other hand, he was pleased with the photograph at last sent by Eduard. Freud sent a poem described jokingly as his "poetic heights" and inspired by a "most extraordinary occasion" (Freud, 1871–1881, pp. 132–133).

1.2   The return of the witch

1.2.1   A threat appears

The letter of 27th February 1875 seems to mark a key moment in both their correspondence and their friendship. For the first time, Freud signed off as "Sigmund", changing the spelling of his given name and avoiding the habitual and cordial "Your Cipion", which concluded his previous letters. This formality followed a more sententious "accept the most cordial greetings", which contrasted with the generally more affectionate tenor of his letters. The present missive adopted a more realistic tone, linked to its subject. Freud was worried and embarrassed; he started his letter by saying how much he appreciated those of his friend's qualities he believed to himself to be lacking: his sense of humour and his poetic genius in dealing with life. He said he had urged his friend to carry out his plan of studying at a German university despite wanting to keep him nearby. He was preparing his following argument, which involved a criticism of Eduard's lifestyle.

While distance and separation provoked contradictory feelings, ambivalence and the disidealisation it entailed created more significant differences between the two. The following example illustrates the complexity of these inner shifts and Freud's struggle with any emotional distance from Eduard. In early 1875, he would still feel a violent jealousy against anyone who, by seducing his friend, might try to come between them. Freud's injury was particularly painful since he saw Eduard's behaviour as a form of betrayal, all the more so because in their imagined life together there was indeed a place for women, but only on the condition that it remained secondary.

And that was certainly not the case for Eduard, when he wrote to Freud about a young lady he met at a dance. Freud's first reaction was to joke that the ballroom event read like a modern French idyll rather than a classical one. The latter would require a blue sky, grazing cattle and sheep, he imagined, "whereas the modern contents itself with black coats, kid gloves, and the pleased expressions of young men and girls. All in all, I have abstracted a prescription for my small psychological medicine chest from it" (p. 83). He then added that if one wished to be in an idyllic mood, one should don tails and white kid gloves to become a big happy child. Yet given that he was no Saint Anthony he should "cut his hectoring" (Ibid.) and ask his friend not to forget to describe the colour of the eyes and the hair of the girl in question. He remarked sarcastically that Eduard seemed to enjoy his dancing lessons more than his other studies – another sign of the differences between them, we might say. In the postscript to one of his subsequent letters, there was something that has occurred to Freud, once freed of the obligation to write. Eduard was in Braila and Freud asked whether there were any "Veronicas"[3] there to dance with. Ironically, but also vengefully, Freud had been telling everyone in their circle that Eduard had become a "wild dancer" (p. 129), so that "males cross themselves at the mention of your name and females are dying with longing to meet you. I hope I have not embarrassed you with this assignment, because it would certainly provide a lot of fun for me", he concluded. After the first letter on the topic, dance was now associated with wild sexual activities from which Freud felt excluded, adding to his ambivalence towards his friend's attempts at seduction.

If we think of adolescence as a radically different process of a subject's social development, we can say that at the age of twenty, Freud had an uncommon degree of intellectual maturity; however, despite his capacities of autonomy, his psychosexual maturity was still apparently fixated on incestual fantasies. This prevented the process of dis-idealisation of the maternal figure, which created an obstacle in trying to encounter young women while maintaining the homosexual intensity of his relationship with Eduard. The temporal lag between these two registers is significant: at the beginning of adolescence, genital sexuality generally manifests much earlier than the first sexual encounters. Likewise, the potential end of adolescence was divided for Freud between his professional achievements on the one hand and his incestuous investments on the other.

1.2.2   An illicit passion

Let's return to the letter of 27th February 1875. Freud's letters on this topic give us some idea of Eduard's response. Based on this, the contrast between them was striking: while Eduard made it clear that he very much enjoyed meeting girls and liked to feel attractive, Freud found the company of the two Fluss sisters a heavy burden. Freud communicated to his friend that the affair was "very wrong of him"; it would cause "grave harm to yourself and deep sorrow to me". It was caused by an "imprudent affection" of a sixteen-year-old, one that threatened Eduard and, were he to take advantage of it, would inevitably bring about a disaster. He did not think Eduard was being "deliberately frivolous", rather he was attracted to the romanticism of the love story or the "unconstrained freedom on both sides, the opposition to the sham and sanctimonious stolidity and insipidity of so-called good society" (Freud, 1871–1881, p. 92). He added, more generally, that their power as young men was before all in "initiating action", implying the commitment entailed in sexual relationships. For Freud, the danger was serious.

Indeed, it did not matter whether his friend's intentions were innocent or "dishonourable" – the consequences would be the same. He then took a more philosophical approach: a man could taste many things but should not cause an injury to himself or provoke long-term unhappiness. The idea of giving in to passion and loosening the reins of morality led him to say, "A thinking man is his own legislator, confessor, and absolver", while a woman and especially a young girl "has no inherent ethical standard" (p. 92). A woman was unable to rebel against conventions without losing her dignity and value, while a man could regain the respect he had lost through work. Freud expressed his fear that Eduard would become the "cause of the first transgression of a young girl – one who has barely outgrown childhood – against a justified moral precept, by arranging meetings and exchanging letters against her parents' wishes". (p. 93). He scolded his friend's vanity, him being too receptive to a sixteen-year-old's charms – a rather paradoxical reproach, given his own infatuation with the thirteen-year-old Gisela.

Eduard's potential correspondence with this young girl was criticised as useless or indeed harmful: "and what purpose will it serve when you lie yourself into a passion and she dreams herself into one?" (p. 93) While Freud appealed to his friend's sense of honour, he nevertheless believed that Eduard had taken the first step along a path towards indignity. This awaited freedom was "dangerous and wanton" for the satisfaction of a "romantic whim". He was aware of his "sermonizing" tone, but still told Eduard to give up his rendezvous and the secret correspondence with a woman depicted as a rival to the exclusivity of their shared secret world. If Eduard could not resist, he should come join him in Vienna: "There you can exchange the normal civilities instead, or swagger about like any student – or do you think you are too good for that?" (p. 93), ultimately exposing Freud's own moral system.

1.2.3 Bad education

Physical distance was also designated as a source of tension: in the imagined conflict of influence, it was him against the alleged seductress, whom Eduard could not resist unless he came home to Freud. He then pushed further: given Eduard's usual abhorrence of flattery, how could he enjoy a situation in which, as it is often the case with girls, his paramour could be spoiled by flattery?

> Every man is, as it were, an educator of all those he meets: by his example, by his behaviour toward them. But you do harm to the poor things when you accustom them to flattery and gallantries that they quickly come to consider as necessities, expecting them as their daily bread and no longer as delicacies. How often have I not complained of the miserable education of girls, deploring their ineptitude for life's serious tasks?
>
> (Ibid.)

After these warning shots, Freud's criticisms only grew bolder, voicing his doubts about a girl he had never actually met. "She cannot even have enjoyed a proper education . . . if she could so easily promise you what you have mentioned." Education was seen as a bastion of virtue, showing that what was at stake was indeed a girl's deflowering. Freud seemed shocked and implored his friend to be careful in partaking in "so dangerous a game". He added the final touch: "How ashamed I would be if you returned to Vienna and I had to keep an episode of your life in Leipzig from our friends and my parents." To which Eduard responded, as surmised from Freud's following letter, that Freud was seeing things unclearly, through the blue spectacles of fantasy. Freud added that the intentions of the girl's mother, a poor silly woman (p. 95), would be to capture the eighteen-year-old Eduard for her daughter. "The old girl is a shrewd woman," acting in her daughter's interest by vaunting the latter's charms and graces. An encounter between two young people at the dance thus became the basis for a much more sophisticated scenario full of persecutory elements. After his investment in the relationship with Gisela-Eleanor, or the image of the mother and her twelve-year-old child from the train episode, this was a new and negative version of the mother-child dyad. Freud was convinced that the dance lesson was the mother's way of encouraging her daughter's coquetry and introduce her into a male society.

1.2.4 A beastly mother

This little story of seduction thus meant that the mother's "trick" had worked, like that of the Witch in *The Dialogue of the Dogs*. Eduard had fallen prey to feminine charms, to "the apparent collusion of mother and daughter" (p. 96). He played the role of a tailor's dummy, Freud wrote, to further discredit the actions of both mother and daughter, who had contaminated and thus feminised Eduard. He tried to protect his friend's narcissism against this "realization", to attenuate his potential injury, by criticising the teenage girl who "has been playing no nobler part" and giving him the role of the "tragic lover". Despite his friend's likely protestations, Freud remained convinced that the girl's mother had deliberately vaunted her daughter's charms to seduce Eduard. His conclusion had to do with the effects of adolescence: "Quite honestly, I would like you the better were you to shed the last remnant of your 'Sturm und Drang'. No doubt you will do that soon without greatly missing it later" (Ibid.).

The criticism did not stop there. In his letter of 13th March 1875, Freud returned to Eduard's description of his first kiss with the girl in a previous letter. The indifference Freud sensed in his friend's depiction was an "evil omen in two respects", namely that his friend "accepts kisses so easily" and also "takes kisses so lightly" (p. 99).

Despite his continuously humourous tone, the following anecdote betrayed his true state of mind: a famous statistician had shown that kisses tended to multiply in proportions that increased with such speed that they are often forced to migrate to other areas of the body. Resuming in a more serious manner, he then accused the girl's mother of being "truly cruel", ruining her daughter by turning her "from a decorous china doll into an indecorous flirt", and urged his friend not to give in to "her plan". The latter seemed truly diabolical, in that it separated the two friends via Eduard's commitment to the girl, while Freud reminded him that in his recent letters he had promised to act differently. The paranoid aspect of this conspiracy depicts the Machiavellian mother as a woman prepared to do whatever it takes to arrange a marriage of interest, a common practice at the time.

While Freud's appeals to Eduard were both unrelenting and direct, this was not the first time he used a moralising and indeed puritanical tone. In the letter dated 22nd August 1874, he presented his conception of morality through literary analysis. He refuted the idea that the immoral was contrary to poetry, but argued: "Rather, poetry, supported by the power of our own passions, can go quite some way toward transfiguring what is immoral, or, better, what society does not allow" (p. 53). He commented on the "impure and loathsome" character of the *Dame aux Camelias*, about which his opinion seemed to oscillate, and concluded that the line between morality and immorality was often difficult to draw.

1.3   Intellectual engagement

1.3.1   *A nationalist bestiary*

While Eduard was busy flirting in Leipzig, during his first university year Freud also joined the *Leseverein der deutschen Studenten Wiens*,[4] a German nationalist group founded in 1871 and disbanded in December 1878 by the authorities for its anti-governmental and anti-Austrian stance. The group specifically supported the German annexation of Austria, discussing ways of overturning the bourgeois world of their allegedly too liberal fathers. Schopenhauer, Wagner and Nietzsche were its spiritual leaders; it aimed to create a new artistically vigorous culture contrasting with the excessive rationalism of the past. The group's political activities revolved around the idea of an integrated man whose rational and emotional sides were no longer separated. Heinrich Braun was elected to the office of the *Leseverein* and in 1877 signed a joint letter to Nietzsche declaring the group's devotion to his ideas; he also suggested to turn the debate towards a critique of liberal society (Trosman, 1973, p. 325).

Freud told Eduard that he had been using the group's library to read Hebbel, for his "harsh and revolutionary nature" (Freud, 1871–1881, p. 107). In his tragedies, a hero fighting for a just cause might die, but his ideas had to triumph or at least not perish. He recommended the five-act tragedy based on the Biblical story of Judith, which he described as staging a "sexual problem" (Ibid.). He then interpreted the story as one of an excessively strong woman defying and taking revenge on an "excessively powerful" man; this revenge was related to the "inferiority her sex has imposed on her". The sexual dimension also appeared in *Ring des Gyges*, which "takes up a sexual problem again" but "often quite charmingly". He concluded that Hebbel's intention was not "to depict women from different points of view or to glorify them politically; rather, he prefers women as the poetically more warm-blooded animals because, in addition to the obstinacy they share with men, they can also have glowing emotions" (p. 108).

On 3rd January 1875, Freud informed Eduard that a common acquaintance, Fleischer, had been expelled from the *Leseverein* due to a scandal. Fleischer played an important role in the Viennese student life but made himself unpopular in his wish to create a unified German state.

On 7th March 1875, Freud wrote about a meeting of the student organisation during which Karl Grün gave a lecture on the three ages of the human spirit. Eduard had previously enjoyed the socialist author's essay on Börne. Freud gave no details as to the contents of the lecture, instead speaking of his passion for the modern "saints" of the natural sciences such as Haeckel, Darwin or Feuerbach. He was pleased with "so steadfast a champion of 'our' truths" (p. 96) and his celebration of students and used the opportunity to criticise those who dismissed the speaker: the little minds of these "future world leaders" were ruled by "a miserable, shallow, urbane and frivolous scepticism".

1.3.2 Some German asses

He again mentioned the Reading Union to praise its patriotic politics and reformatory zeal. He initially signed the petition to withdraw membership from the industrialist Victor Ofenheim, who was accused, despite his eventual acquittal, by the conservative and anti-Semitic voices of being responsible for the stock exchange collapse of 1873. Freud adhered to this opinion, voiced in a recent speech by a Dr Volkelt, whose work on *Dream Imagination* was later cited repeatedly in the *Interpretation on Dreams*. The Reading Union published his speech, which allowed Freud to now send it to Eduard, to pass it on to the social democrats in his circle and continue the discussion between the two of them (Freud, 1871–1881, p. 112).

His tone was less cutting, as illustrated by the signature: "accept the cordial greetings of your Sigismund". Ending on a less passionate note, the letter marked a greater distance between them. In the post-script he once again demanded a photograph, joking that he no longer remembered what his friend, for whom social democrats and the republic are vying, looked like – an allusion to the effects of their separation. No surprise then that it took seventeen days before the next letter, which Freud apologised for profusely, afraid to set a bad example as a friend. Setting an example was indeed what Freud seemed used to in his friendships, as an extension of his family ties, especially vis-à-vis his siblings but also his parents. He thought of his friend more than ever and could not wait to see him the following winter, instead of just writing letters every other week, i.e., much less frequently than in the early days of the Spanish Academy.

Despite belonging to a nationalist grouping, Freud declared himself a republican, considering the republic "the only sensible, indeed self-evident, system", but also rejecting any revolutionary attempt to establish such a republic. He added, in view of his real commitments: "I should be very interested to hear whether your social democrats are revolutionary in the philosophical and religious spheres as well" – given that in his own daydreams of ambition, he wanted to bring about a revolution. It was from this perspective that one could see whether the social democrats close to his friend's heart were truly radical or not. Like every other time he would question Eduard's beliefs – about the girl at the ball, or his political or philosophical convictions – Freud would subsequently soften his tone, to say that he had nothing against his socialist aspirations when it came to improving education, the struggle for existence or the distribution of property.

On 18th December 1876, Freud sent a postcard mentioning the Union for the last time. He asked his friend to join him at the "meeting of the German asses" (p. 163), an allusion to *Leseverein*, since "ass" in university slang referred to a student.

Shortly before what has sometimes been called the Freudian Revolution, Freud still dreamt about this Union, some twenty-five years after its disbanding. In a letter to Martha, he wrote that at a party he talked about the war with Gilles de la Tourette, telling him he felt neither German nor Austrian but a Jew. He added that this type of conversation was always disagreeable to him, "for I feel stirring within me something German which I long ago decided to suppress" (Freud, 1873–1939, p. 203).

1.3.3   Dreaming of a revolution

The membership of the Union did leave a mark on Freud, and he returns to this episode of his student life in the dream of the Count Thun:

> The dream as a whole gives one the impression of being in the nature of a phantasy in which the dreamer was carried back to the Revolutionary year 1848. Memories of that year had been recalled to me by the [Emperor Francis Joseph's] Jubilee in 1898.
>
> (Freud, 1900, p. 211)

The name of the movement's leader, Fischof, brings up another series of associations, with his brother in England, who liked to tease his wife with the words "Fifty years ago", from the title of Tennyson's poems. Alexander Freud's children would then correct him by saying "fift*een* years ago", which creates an association for Freud between the idea of a revolution and the age of fifteen. This link between a father and his teenage children confirms Freud's identification with his brother, while in his dreams he also discovers a series of associations with his teenage sons (Houssier, Chagnon, 2016).

The revolutionary connotations of this dream find a precise connection with the student Union, which Freud points out apropos a dream of German posters on the walls of Rome, where the fulfilment of his wish to travel to Rome is combined with a memory of "a German-nationalist phase which I passed through during my youth" (Freud, 1900, p. 323).

This intense albeit short-lived experience is also present in another dream, which goes back to the period when Freud still socialised with Braun and met Viktor Adler during a lively debate.

> Behind this lay a recollection of a piece of antisemitic provocation during a railway journey in the lovely Saxon countryside (cf. Anglo-Saxon). – The third scene which contributed to the formation of the first situation in the dream dated from my early student days. There was a discussion in a German students' club on the relation of philosophy to the natural sciences. I was a green youngster, full of materialistic theories, and thrust myself forward to give expression to an extremely one-sided point of view.
>
> (Freud, 1900, p. 212)

The discussion was with Adler, and Freud pays him a discreet homage, criticising his own attitude:

> Thereupon someone who was my senior and my superior, someone who has since then shown his ability as a leader of men and an organizer of large groups (and who also, incidentally, bears a name derived from the Animal Kingdom), stood up and gave us a good talking-to: he too, he told us, had fed swine in his youth and returned repentant to his father's house. I fired up (as I did in the dream) and replied boorishly ['saugrob', literally 'swinishly gross'] that since I now knew that he had fed swine in his youth I was no longer surprised at the tone of his speeches. (In the dream I was surprised at my German-nationalist attitude.)
>
> (p. 212–213)

We notice that the controversy starts from the idea of a humble return to the father, which seems to make Freud want to pick up a fight and, in his anger, he uses invectives. The idea of a wrongful independence from his father is upsetting to young Freud. The anger expressed is not the only emotion linked to nationalism; nationalist pride again returns at the onset of WWI and only then is abandoned.

Let's return to the debate with Adler, which ends in verbal fisticuffs:

> There was a general uproar and I was called upon from many sides to withdraw my remarks, but I refused to do so. The man I had insulted was too sensible to look upon the incident as a challenge, and let the affair drop.
>
> (Ibid.)

And that is the end of it. In the associations with the dream, we should notice that the scene involves a collection of insults all referring to animals: giraffe, monkey, pig, swine, dog, donkey. The last one is again associated with a provocation: "I could have arrived at 'donkey' if I had made a *detour* through another name and insulted yet another academic teacher." The dog brings up the association between three terms: impropriety, the approaching revolution and "the production of a gaseous excretion known by the name of 'flatus'" (Ibid.). These images give the dream the value of a memory: the inability to contradict his father in the summer of 1873 is replaced by a virulent opposition towards authority figures, even at the price of creating an uproar. The critical murder of the paternal figure is combined with a kind of megalomania: the anality of his provocation is linked to the idea of a revolution, which requires killing the father by overturning the established order.

1.3.4   How to be young

In the final stages of Freud and Eduard's epistolary relationship, the letter of 7th September 1877 revisits their shared acquaintances. Freud learnt that Braun had been in Vienna but did not contact him, which provoked the somewhat bitter remark: "This is an example of how old attachments can evaporate" (Freud, 1871–1881, p. 166).

He spoke about the festive High Holiday meal, which burdened his stomach with greater girth and an increased consumption of acid, adding: "We young people who have half left our own families and have not yet found a new one are in fact singularly unsuited to the enjoyment of holidays" (p. 167). The last sentence again alluded to his idea of youth and specifically of student life.

Speaking about himself, he wrote that as a child he firmly believed in the envy of the so-called gods (p. 86) and would take care not to speak of any wishes in order not to "invoke the very opposite". But now the world was looking "brighter" and the potential of fulfilling his wishes brought him his "greatest joy" (Ibid.). The prolonging of his adolescence became a time of potential self-realisation.

The moralising tone then returned. "La Ac. Esp. requests that you . . . have a good yawn first, so that your letter evinces the youthful vigor and strength of purpose that becomes a finished Gymnasium scholar and future citizen of Academe"

(p. 51). Later, the letter dated 8th November 1875 began with a mood report; Freud described a "sad week" during which "a wintery mood has descended upon me" (p. 70). He resolved to take better care of his "physical well-being" through walks and other outings. He used this opportunity to philosophise about the immortal soul and the body which needed looking after. "Have you never heard that we only live once?", he railed against his friend's overloaded schedule, which was a concern for himself as well.

When Eduard decided to work alongside his studies to gain more financial independence from his father, Freud positioned himself as an authority rather than an equal, acting as both a psychologist and an educator. He emphasised that, knowing Eduard's father, the latter had sent his son to study abroad wanting him to enjoy himself and the occasional expense would not be a heavy sacrifice.

He tried to dissuade Eduard from giving private lessons for extra income; he praised "the specific aroma of student life" (p. 60). Being a student meant being "master of one's own time" and enjoying one's freedom; on the other hand, tutoring would reduce Eduard's life to "slavery". While he regularly expressed resentment and sometimes pain about his own modest circumstances, he reassured his friend that neither riding nor fencing would be a financial obstacle for Eduard's father. He wrote, this time expressing his deepest thoughts:

I cannot understand the feverish haste with which you want to escape your youth. Remember that, once grown up and professionally trained, you will be subjected to a thousand demands by your present family and the one you have still to acquire, by domestic and public life, and perhaps by your academic work as well. If you enjoy the pursuit of your studies in the stillness of your own thoughts and feelings and the undisturbed pleasure in yourself that the division of interests and multiplication of cares will never grant you again in later life, then make use of the time set aside for that purpose by your parents and everyone else; for once youth has fled people will tend to begrudge you every moment you devote to your own pursuits.

The idea of enjoying the present moment, which returned after he met Martha, emerges here clearly. He continued:

If, however, it is your highest aim to live for others, then remember that everything you now do for yourself will later benefit other people, and grant you the double satisfaction of perfecting yourself while being able to work for them. In any case – use your time for your own good; youth is but the close season in which destiny allows us to gain strength so that we can amuse her by our resistance if she later decides to hunt us down.

(p. 61)

This was the eighteen-year-old Freud's philosophy of youth; he also warned that giving lessons would not in fact earn Eduard "mountains of gold".

He used several metaphors to imagine his statistics teacher, once also a young man, "as a freshman, the maternal eggshell of the Gymnasium still stuck to his back". He too must have studied something else besides "the arid stuff". Freud asked his friend to tell him more about his "more intimate" everyday life and intellectual interests. Indeed, this is what he was trying to offer Eduard – a more intimate view of his adolescence, similar to his own experience. On this level, Freud's own personal development no doubt contributed to a certain emotional estrangement between the two young men.

1.3.5   The Brentano experience

According to Boelich (1990), Freud's passion for literature, which regularly featured in his psychoanalytic texts, was greatly enriched by his study of philosophy. He studied the subject together with his friend Josef Paneth, who personally met Nietzsche in 1883 and told Freud about it (Eissler, 1955). In 1934, Freud commented on this in a letter to Arnold Zweig: "In my youth he was a remote and noble figure to me. A friend of mine, Dr. Paneth, had got to know him in the Engadine and had written a lot to me about him." However, Freud denied that the philosopher would have had any influence on his own thinking.

The two friends sent two letters to Brentano to communicate their objections to his philosophical theory. In return, they were twice invited to the professor's home. Brentano made such an impression on Freud that he wrote to Silberstein he was thinking of doing his doctorate in both philosophy and zoology. Brentano made Freud – a young Jew and an atheist – consider the existence of god, even though Feuerbach's influence on him was probably much greater. In the latter case too, Freud refused of any such possible influence. In a 1925 letter to Binswanger, he wrote that Brentano did not have a lasting influence on him, which we can consider debatable. Boehlich believes that Freud did not want psychoanalysis to be associated with any specific philosophical current, even though Feuerbach's work was possibly one source of his criticism of religion and may have even contributed to the fundamental discovery of psychoanalysis.

Freud thus attended Brentano's lectures from 1874 to 1876, especially his courses on Aristotle. Brentano also recommended Freud to his colleague Theodor Gomperz as a translator for the twelfth volume of John Stuart Mill's works. In 1913, Freud wrote a letter to Gomperz's widow, which gives us some indications of Gomperz's importance to him:

The little notebook containing the handwriting of your unforgotten husband reminded me of that time lying so far behind us, when I, young and timid, was allowed for the first time to exchange a few words with one of the great men in the realm of thought. It was soon after this that I heard from him the first remarks about the role played by dreams in the psychic life of primitive men – something that has preoccupied me so intensively ever since.

(Freud, 1873–1939, p. 303)

As to Mill, Freud was highly critical of him, denouncing his lifeless style and lack of originality in a letter to Martha (Ibid., p. 75). However, after reading one of his philosophical works, he later concluded that Mill may have been "the man of the century most capable of freeing himself from the domination of the usual prejudices".

According to Roudinesco (2016), Freud and his friend Josef Paneth challenged Brentano's theism by invoking the materialism of Feuerbach, whose philosophy proclaimed the return to concrete humanity and criticised the alienation of transcendence. Feuerbach's sensualism and criticism of religion inspired Freud to reject the field of philosophy as too abstract and theological.

The fight against Brentano therefore led to Freud's decision to give up his pursuit of philosophy. "But since his fondness for denying himself pleasures freed him to gain access to what he considered essential on his own terms, he continued to let himself be seduced by speculative thought", Roudinesco writes, pointing out that abstract thought was never absent from Freud's method and in fact permeated his entire work. I would rather argue that this speculative tendency, which is characteristic of all teenagers in their willingness to transform the world, was a source of tension in Freud's work, between "giving in" to irrational ideas and maintaining the scientific orientation of psychoanalysis against all odds, for example around the question of parapsychology or the desexualisation of the libido.

1.3.6   *Psychology, in particular*

Let's see what he actually wrote about this to Eduard. At the beginning of the exam period, Freud's letter of 7th March 1975 sounded much calmer. He complained about the lengthy semesters, which were dragging on, preventing him from enjoying "the freedom of the vacation" (Freud, 1871–1881, p. 94). He compared these to a limb that "dies off at a time and one is tempted to finish off those that go on twitching". He also spoke about his and Paneth's interactions with Brentano and the philosopher's lectures, which led them to write to him with a number of scientific objections. The professor, whom he described as a philosopher, teleologist, Darwinist, greatly intelligent or even a genius – an ideal – was very approachable and invited them to come and talk to him about their arguments. Under his influence, which Freud considered fruitful, he had now decided to take his doctorate in philosophy and to study zoology at the philosophical faculty the following year.

The story of meeting Brentano with Paneth was an opportunity to present his own scientific positions. Against Brentano's empiricism, he defined himself as a materialist, applying the scientific method to philosophy and "to psychology in particular" (p. 102). After the long description of their discussion with Brentano and the philosophers the latter either criticised or recommended, Freud concluded that Eduard might feel flattered to have a friend "thought worthy of the company of so excellent a man" (p. 104). Freud had not escaped Brentano's influence, especially in being unable to refute his simple theistic argument. However, it is his description of his personality that tells us more about what Freud appreciated: "he abhors all glib phrases, all emotionality, and all intolerance of other views". The portrait conveys an admiration that foretells Freud's future reorientation towards science, not only in terms of his specific interest for psychology, but also his relationship to scientific demonstration: "He demonstrates the existence of God with as little bias and as much precision as another might argue the advantage of the wave over the emission theory" (Ibid.). While he wished to go deeper into Brentano's philosophy to gain a more exact and thorough opinion of it, he wrote that he was no longer a materialist and not yet a theist. He would have liked to align his belief in Darwinism (criticised by Brentano) with his teleology, which considered God as a "logically necessary scientific hypothesis" (p. 111). He expanded on this by making a comparison between his friend's political questioning (republicanism or socialism) and his own (theism or materialism). Repentant, he spoke about hardcore materialism as lacking in "philosophical insight". His decision had not yet been made and kept changing, especially apropos the knowledge he did not yet have (p. 110). He also tried to reassure his friend by saying that he was far from indifferent to his social questions, even though he mostly grasped them through Eduard's perspective. What repelled him was the social democrats' dogmatism and intolerance: "certainly not the right way to attract adherents from the learned estate" (Ibid.).

The letter of 27th March 1875 was highly self-critical, in a way that necessarily reminds us of Freud's future self-analysis. He had been too dogmatic and logical, believing in his favourite theories, while today his "secret leaning toward minority views has grown", expanding his thought (p. 106). However, under the influence of Brentano or Eduard, who sent him ten pages on homeopathy, this leaning could lead him to believe in spiritism or in the stigmata of Louise Lateau,[5] one of his contemporaries. Freud was also surprised that the conversation with Brentano was in fact able to change his way of thinking, especially in terms of religion; he was afraid he might be too suggestible and open to all kinds of arguments in these and other fields. He also came to another important conclusion: to really understand a theory, one must study it thoroughly, in depth and detail. This later resulted in his psychological research method, constructing his theory of dreams from personal, clinical and literary material. This open-minded approach nevertheless had its limits. For instance, Freud was highly critical of a theatre play he had recently seen and could not appreciate "for the intricate and dangerous psychological experiments it portrays have something improbable about them" (p. 108). This was one way of struggling against speculation – to see the studied object as improbable or fantastic. The conflict between speculation and rationality, his two opposing tendencies, therefore indeed emerged following the discussions with Brentano. Just like on other occasions, this conflict was only rarely denied and found a point of connection with Freud's irrational and incestuous investments, and his rationalist struggle against these hidden desires.

1.3.7   *Matter,* **mutter,** *mother*

Freud's father wanted him to become the businessman he himself never was, and in July 1875 Sigmund left for Manchester. He later wrote that since his time as an eighteen-year-old in England his imagination became fixated on the country and he wished to become an Englishman (Freud, 1873–1939, p. 459). The story he tells in his book on dreams (Freud, 1900, p. 519) includes another anecdote:

> When I was nineteen years old I visited England for the first time and spent a whole day on the shore of the Irish Sea. I naturally revelled in the opportunity of collecting the marine animals left behind by the tide and I was occupied with a starfish – the words "*Hollthurn*" and "*holothurians* [sea-slugs]" occurred at the beginning of the dream – when a charming little girl came up to me and said: "Is it a starfish? Is it alive?" "Yes," I replied, "he is alive," and at once, embarrassed at my mistake, repeated the sentence correctly. The dream replaced the verbal error which I then made by another into which a German is equally liable to fall. "*Das Buck ist von Schiller*" should be translated not with a "from" but with a "by". After all that we have heard of the purposes of the dream-work and its reckless choice of methods for attaining them, we shall not be surprised to hear that it effected this replacement because of the magnificent piece of condensation that was made possible by the identity of sound of the English "from" and the German adjective "*fromm*" ["pious"].

The deconstruction of the dream continues as follows:

> But how did my blameless memory of the sea-shore come to be in the dream? It served as the most innocent possible example of my using a word indicating gender or sex in the wrong place – of my bringing in sex (the word "he") where it did not belong. This, incidentally, was one of the keys to the solution of the dream. No one who has heard, furthermore, the origin attributed to the title of Clerk Maxwell's "*.Matter* and *Motion*" will have any difficulty in filling in the gaps: Molière's "Le *Malade* Imaginaire" – "La *matière* est-elle laudable?" – A motion of the bowels.

This time, England had to do not with his father but his mother. The sex of the starfish, as that of the eels, was discovered here as male, which brings the idea of bringing his genitals where they did not belong. These comments seem part of the bisexual fantasy we have already identified in relation to the blonde bisexual angel from the Vienna train station in Freud's letter to Fluss (Houssier, 2018a).

In his letter of 28th June 1875, Freud responded to Eduard's reproach that he was spreading himself too thin among too many different subjects. He was not unaware of it and wanted to give up on his idea of studying physical optics during his holidays. In these generally shorter letters before the beginning of the summer, when he informed Eduard of his planned journey in July, we see Freud writing "Your

Sigmund" and "Eduard" or "Dear friend" (as opposed to *Berganza*). He began his letter of 3rd August by excusing himself for not having written earlier, "as if he had been swallowed up by the waves of the Germanic sea" (Freud, 1871–1881, p. 123). He wrote about his family in England, his "beautiful nieces" and the "places of entertainment" he saw in the streets of Manchester – all this was "new" to him. He had "better things to do" than writing letters, except to Eduard; nevertheless, the Castilian used in the letter was "no more than the ruins" of the Spanish Academy. This lament continued in the following letter, where he wrote he had decided to procure himself a Spanish dictionary to help him write in the language that Eduard had again started to use. Remembering their shared studies and walks, he wrote that each of them loved the other as a complete person, rather than, as it was the case before, solely for their good qualities. Even if Eduard turned out to be unworthy of this love, Freud would still keep wishing him well – but this was a weakness on his part, and he reproached himself for it.

He then spoke about his Manchester family, especially his "two charming nieces" (Ibid., p. 127), including the nineteen-year-old Pauline. He was coming back from his trip with "more than one ideal", having added a practical ideal to the theoretical one of the past years. Previously, this ideal boiled down to a wish to have a laboratory and everything a researcher would need, while now he would rather say "a large hospital and plenty of money in order to reduce or wipe out some of the ills that afflict our body" (Ibid.). England would be just the place for this purpose, for such "ambition". "A respected man, supported by the press and the rich, could do wonders in alleviating physical ills, if only he were enough of an explorer to strike out on new therapeutic paths." Freud returned home with a favourable view of the English scientists; England was associated with the professional success of his two half-brothers. Yet his medical ambitions were combined with a contrary feeling, of being "more suspicious than ever of philosophy" (p. 128), despite Brentano's revelations, a kind of magical parenthesis in his scientific journey. At this moment, his interest in psychology seems to have faded somewhat.

In his letter of 19th September 1875, he worried that when Eduard would come to Vienna, he would be very busy with "no less than eight examinations" (p. 129). When thinking of the workload awaiting him, all that he had set up to occupy himself with in Eduard's absence suddenly seemed to turn against their friendship.

1.4   The end of a friendship

1.4.1   A question of security

Speaking about his upcoming birthday and Eduard's arrival in Vienna, Freud's tone grew more sober. The romantic walks of yesteryear were replaced by a wish to "[be] peacefully united in the Prater or the City Park in the land of milk and honey" (Freud, 1871–1881, p. 119), referring to the sweets sold in these popular city spots. The sugary atmosphere reminiscent of childhood and the maternal world was nevertheless somewhat marred by Freud's preoccupations. He could not help himself but continue questioning his friend about his "heroic principle", a young girl who had again come between them.

In relation to a relatively anecdotic event, where someone threw a stone through the window of the family home, leaving "a nice round hole – nothing else", Freud imagined "the pleasure of being a minister or professor in bad times and possessing a few more windows" (p. 114). This fear of persecution also suggests a possible shift: the wish to become a minister could be replaced with becoming a professor, both vocations connoting a sense of security, including financial security. Freud added: "But let us take solace: everything is but a passage, as was once inscribed on a bridge, 'passage,' although to what no one can tell" (p. 114).

The letter of 17th May 1875, written in Spanish following the Academy's codes, was a protest against what Freud saw as his friend's nearly month-long absence, begging him to "break your silence forthwith" (Ibid., p. 115). Freud had learnt from his brother that Eduard was well and wrote to his parents regularly, hence the resentment. He had imagined that Eduard's silence meant he may have been killed in a duel and wanted to know what was happening, signing off as "entirely yours", after promising Eduard that he only needed to come to Vienna "and you will find me, I assure you".

In the following letter of 13th June 1875 Freud made his amends and recognised that his studies had in turn prevented him from answering more speedily. When Eduard suggested Freud go to see one of his friends, Klamper, whom he had met briefly, he rejected this new idea of a third. He had no time – but also there was Klamper's mental state. He disagreed with Eduard that he should be engaging more with Klamper's period of melancholy and weariness. To justify himself, he wrote that these types of melancholic states only rarely resulted in cases of insanity and suicide; the lack of friends was not among the young man's problems. However, he did make a gesture by asking Eduard to prepare the ground, so that he and Klamper could speak freely to each other. To further his own agenda, he wrote that when one was depressed, one needed one's best friends to confide in, but also that Klamper's secrets revolved solely around his mental pain, rather than his joys or passions, while Freud could do both: complain and share his happy moments. Klamper returned in the letter of 2nd October 1875; Freud had written to him before the holidays and then had no time to see him; but if everything had gone according to Klamper's plans, he should now be in the army. In any case, Freud remained markedly ambivalent regarding Eduard's worries about Klamper.

While a sense of rivalry was still a burning issue, Freud said he had little to write about himself, which was unusual, especially because his letter followed nearly a month after his previous one. This general distancing also had to do with another point of disagreement. Freud remained committed to science: over the summer holidays, he wanted to study histology and zoology using a small microscope and a small chemical laboratory. However, "with you, politics seems to have ousted science completely", he commented, warning Eduard not to "capitulate to the social democrats body and soul" (Ibid., p. 118).

1.4.2   Having a friend in one's pocket

In the letter of 19th September 1875, Freud worried he might be too busy with exams when Eduard returned to Vienna. The fact of jumping from one topic to another made him think he had little to say to his friend – a comment caught up in the contradiction between wishing to revive their Academy and the gradual disinvestment of their friendship. Passion in a friendship and even more so in a relationship with a "principle" was often experienced by him as an obstacle to fulfilling his ambitions, diverting him from his path. With Eduard, passion did not fade away smoothly; Freud spoke about his "extremely disagreeable" disappointment (p. 61) when he received his friend's letter suggesting that Eduard was bored and had nothing special to report. He again appealed to the notion of duty, telling his friend off for such a brief and indifferent letter. He felt betrayed by what he saw as a lack of interest. A letter like this could not compensate for his friend's absence or his long silence; finally, he concluded that it was a sign that Eduard was turning away from him, and writing had become a burden. This time, he defined his idea of a friend was someone "self-possessed", who would always find something interesting to say, or something that caused him doubt and would make him call upon friends for reassurance. Often "selfless sympathy" was "indeed the sole contribution of a friend", but also the most valuable. And writing to a friend did not require a special mood. The often-jocular form of his letters "does not mean that I wish to turn my letter into a madhouse" (p. 62). His friend's wit and irony were important to him, especially his humour.

Possibly aware of the power of his criticism, Freud's tone then softened, reminding Eduard that writing without duress was one of the Academy's rules, and that the form was of little consequence. Their journal could be filled with a "learned treatise or a few thoughts worthy of Werther". The reference to Goethe's novel *The Sorrows of Young Werther* is not without importance – Freud appealed to the tragic romantism of the work, identifying with its author.

Other moments also betray the growing ambivalence in their friendship. Freud's struggles in sending a letter necessarily remind us of some of his arguments in the *Psychopathology of Everyday Life* apropos bungled actions (Freud, 1901b). Having written the letter, he kept it in his pocket for three days "like a marsupial harboring its young on its body after birth" (Freud, 1871–1881, p. 72). He then put it in an envelope, but another problem appeared: he could not remember his friend's address. He then could not manage to post it or, as he suggests, could not separate himself from it. The letter represented both Eduard, from whom he did not wish to separate, but also a maternal bond in which his friend had to be kept close to his body despite – or perhaps because – of his autonomy. Keeping him warm like a mother keeps a baby illustrated the relationship of dependence Freud so strongly desired.

To excuse his "distraction", he spoke about the impulses of memory that could be attributed to a "poor troubled medical student" (Ibid., p. 73). We see isolation, solitude and a heavy workload, with no love on the horizon, a sense of resignation – all of these contributed to Freud's unhappiness. As if to signal to his friend that he wished they were on the same page emotionally, he also spoke about the niece and bride of Mr Herzig, adding: "I am confident that you, like me, much prefer to be still looking for your future bride than to have her around every day and hour" (p. 106).

1.4.3   Feeling forgotten

At a later point, after Eduard's repeated complaints about the loss of a text on "pearls or marguerites", Freud's attitude to his friend again became harsh and judgmental. He looked for the text, unsuccessfully, but believed that the pearls were not "worth seeking or bemoaning, so worthless and devoid of talent are they" (Ibid., p. 97). Adding insult to injury, he then wrote that Eduard might have remembered the text with so much enthusiasm because it was linked to his memories of his school days, even though other things could remind him of this time as well and "it is advisable to allow the pearls to sink into the ocean of oblivion. That is all I have to say in reply to your ultimatum", he concluded. This moment in their correspondence suggests that Freud's reaction was all the stronger because of their painful separation. His intellectual hyper-maturity became a pretext for his domineering attitude towards Eduard, as we see in his criticism of his friend's writing.

The hope of reviving their friendship was nevertheless still present. The end of the letter touched on the secret language of their Academy. The code substituted certain words for others, for instance referring to a dead person as someone who has "departed from Seville" or to someone travelling from Vienna to Berlin as changing their "thickness". Loss and separation were at the heart of these linguistic displacements, from a German-speaking country to another, Spain, and its legendary cities: Seville, Cadiz and Madrid, the Academy's promised land.

After he had already criticised Eduard's romantic choices, Freud goes still further in the letter of 13th August 1876, asking whether Eduard had become a martyr and would like to be canonised, having sacrificed his health on the altar of his studies. According to Freud, Eduard was studying all kinds of things "without rhyme or reason" (Ibid., p. 157) – a criticism that could well be applied to himself.

The letter, which Freud had been writing for three days without being able to finish, mentioned several other events. His mother and sisters had spoken "marvels" about Eduard. However, a new ambivalent interruption arrived when Freud spilled half a glass of water on the letter, which explained the illegibility of certain passages. "To crown it all", he imagined that Eduard might not receive the letter at all and believe that Freud had forgotten him and his friendship duties – thus returning his own reproach to his supposedly too cavalier friend against himself.

He also responded to Eduard's request to send him a bow for a violin, but warned him to use it sparingly, due to his frail health and – he could not help but make a joke – because every time Eduard played, his left ear would start ringing.

Freud's attitude reminds us of his analysis of the so-called hypocritical dreams (1900, p. 476). One of his own dreams staged a reconciliation with a friend he had dropped a long time ago. He wrote: "In such cases analysis habitually reveals some occasion which might urge me to abandon the last remnant of consideration for these former friends and to treat them as strangers or enemies", despite the dream's apparently contrary scenario.

1.4.4   A sad and dreary world

Was this linked to the growing distance between them? To Freud's own solitude? When he said he no longer slept for more than four hours a day, spending his nights reading *Don Quixote*, Freud described himself as nervous, languid and bored, feeling like "my limbs had been glued together and were now coming apart again", a kind of painful and embarrassed hangover. This condition had made him avoid lectures and laboratory work for several days, which he instead spent roaming the streets of Vienna, "studying the masses". After a few better nights and lazy days, he then felt good enough to resume work, but decided to reduce the scope of his studies. Rather than "principles", he attributed his state of mind to their absence: "the old ones are no good any longer and no new ones have been found – it is just a time of transition" (p. 89).

Later, he wrote that boredom had made him decide to start keeping a diary, which, akin to his present circumstances, was "rather bleak and uninteresting" (p. 167). The postscript too betrayed his depressive mood: after his many requests that his letters were read carefully, he concluded by saying that it did not matter if Eduard could read it or not.

This was the final year of Freud's studies, but he felt "very lonely, like the last rose of summer" (p. 172), alluding to Moore's poem. He consoled himself with the news of a positive review of his first scientific publication, an article dealing with his zoological research in Trieste. He was cited as the "aforementioned research scientist" and surprised by this compliment from people "who would take the food from each other's mouth" (Ibid.).

In the letter of 10th August 1879, he talked about his recent translation of a John Stuart Mill essay on Plato. He feared that the devil might bring him relatives making demands on his time, which had now become more valuable than ever before. He felt deprived of the "noble Spanish language", with Eduard spending time in Bad Ischl, a fashionable Austrian resort.

Swimming – he mentioned the Prater lido – was regularly on his mind when he felt depressed about a separation, both from Eduard and later from Martha. Sadness, feelings of entrapment and solitude conjured the idea of the swimming pool as a ray of sunshine in his days. Like mountaineering, swimming was tainted with nostalgia of the now past time of his studies; in a similarly sad and lonely mood, Freud also wrote to Eduard that being in touch with nature was "once all that we desired" (Houssier, 2017b).

1.4.5   First analysis of a young girl

Despite these painful moments, Freud's interest in psychological investigations returned in the letter of 25th August 1876, apropos a situation concerning Eduard's younger sister. He began by describing her character: she was "a thoroughly healthy, talented child, though precocious and unbridled as well" (Freud, 1871–1881, Ibid., p. 161), which explained why she naturally rebelled against "the procedures that make up our education". We learn that she had been sent away to a boarding school and, according to Freud's interpretation, it was freedom she lacked the most. He described the young girl's sense of strategy with some admiration: if she tried to insinuate that she could not stay at the school, "it is only to scheme with a will and skill that are rare in one of her age".

During their most recent meeting, he observed her carefully and saw that she looked just as well and appeared just as boisterous as before. Still, he saw it fit to "curb her by institutional discipline" and not give in to her demands to be boarding with a family. He added:

> But your mother is right in not wishing to exert continuous pressure, which could only have a deleterious effect on a child so constituted, and in not wanting [to break] a will that springs from the irreproachable youthful conviction that freedom is better than the classroom.
>
> (p. 161)

Speaking at first from a position of authority, he approached the matter pedagogically but, taking into account the girl's personality, said that if she indeed showed aversion to this "enforced stay" her wishes should be respected.

He also disagreed with Eduard, who he believed would have liked to "keep her in an incubator for refined young ladies" (p. 161–2). To justify his point of view, he added:

> But education must always be considered a boon by the pupil and may be enforced only while there is still hope that he may come to acknowledge it as a boon. Please forgive these lines brought about by your letter to my mother. Do write me something less businesslike from Braila soon. Your Cipion ó Sigmund Freud.

Freud's position shows the tension between a need for more freedom and the educational constraints of his time.

The letter of 15th August 1877 began with Freud's enthusiasm about Eduard's latest romantic idyll – contrary to the jealous scene involving mother and daughter two years previously. He then returned to his recent meeting with Eduard's sister Minna: she seemed well, more grown up and while at first unruly, she later calmed down. She seemed to share the characteristic of all Silbersteins: "to suffer from a surfeit of energy until you are fifteen". She was happy with his gift of several books, especially *The Dream Ladder*, a collection of Andreas's fairy tales published in 1832.

1.4.6 A young scientist discovers hypnosis

Work had now taken up an important place in Freud's life and sometimes compensated for his feelings of solitude. His letters became less frequent and less passionate. In the letter of 14th August 1878, Freud was surprised that Eduard complained of being bored in Braila but had not yet come and seen him during the holiday period. He told him about his visit at the laboratory of the neuropathologist Stricker. He was worried he would never make a real discovery, given the competition and the risk of being overtaken by others researching a popular topic. In terms of his laboratory work, he wanted to study the nerves of salivary glands in dogs.

The postcard of 3rd February 1880 was written in English: Freud wrote about the hypnotist Carl Hansen, whose demonstration he had already seen. This time, instead of revisiting the spectacle, he thought another such evening would "destroy my artificial systematic structure of study". He joked that Eduard should make Hansen come when Freud was a little more "independent" (Freud, 1871–1881, p. 177) and give him his regards; he added that he hoped Eduard would remain sceptical after seeing hypnosis and remember that the exclamation "wonderful" was a sign of ignorance rather than a miracle. "Yours for ever, Sigmund Freud", he signed off this time.

Freud later mentioned Hansen's demonstration in his autobiographical study (1925), where he wrote that it had convinced him of the existence and utility of hypnosis. We again see that some experiences of his youth were firmly inscribed in his mind and did not fade with time, as shown by his own use of hypnosis alongside Breuer, which forged the future practice of psychoanalysis. On this occasion, scientific scepticism outweighed the thrill of the spectacle, but looking back the memory was much less ambivalent. Freud remembered that the evening forged an unshakeable belief in hypnosis in him, long before his time in France and his meeting with Charcot or Bernheim.

The postcard that followed, dated 26th March 1880, was written during the exam period, before Freud announced in his following letter that he had passed his second theoretical examination. He said that he had been worried, having had no time for pharmacology until the day before, but in the end all was well. He now wanted to go to Semmering "with two roses" – his sister and a cousin. He was tired, feeling all the work he had done in his aching limbs. He received his doctoral diploma on 31st March 1881.

In the letter of 3rd October 1880 – we see the long gap that now separated the letters – he told Eduard he had broken two of his best teeth, which would cost a great deal to repair. That was why he skipped a meeting suggested by Eduard, to play cards at a café. He instead offered to come see him at his home, also because he wanted to avoid running into Paneth. On this day, he also announced the beginning of another passion: he had taken to smoking a pipe.

The last letter of his adolescence was dated 24th January 1881; he was nearly twenty-five. He had lost another week to his doctoral exam. He announced the marriage of one of his nieces. "You are invited to come over one of these evenings, as I shall always be at home. With greetings I remain your faithful Cipion" (Freud, 1871–1881, p. 181) is thus the concluding sentence of this correspondence. However, thanks to a number of other letters, we know that their relationship was not completely over.

1.4.7   "I was in love with none and am now with one"

Three years after the end of this correspondence, in his letter to Martha dated 7th February 1884, Freud indicated that he had just seen Silberstein that day and that he felt just as devoted to him as ever. In this first moment of reflection on their past relationship he described his friend as someone who intellectually did not like soaring very high, who was a bit of a philistine and bourgeois but with whom he was never bored. He remembered a farewell party for Eduard, where the latter invited all his former colleagues and himself poured the beer to hide how moved he was. Later at the café, Freud broke the ice by making a speech on behalf of everyone present, in which he said that Eduard would take their youth with him. At first, Freud continued to write to him, urging him to escape his father and instead set up in Bucharest, trying to appeal to his romantic and poetic sensibilities. He remembered all that they had once shared: poetry, sailor stories and Cooper's *Leatherstocking*. A year earlier, Silberstein had a boat on the Danube and let himself call the *Captain*, inviting all his friends on rowing trips.

> Then you appeared on the scene and everything that came with you; a new friend, new struggles, new aims. The drifting apart which had gradually developed between us became apparent again when I advised him from Wandsbek against marrying a stupid rich girl whom he had been sent to have a look at. And then we lost contact with each other.
>
> (Freud, 1873–1939, p. 97)

Freud had used the same word, "stupid", about the young girl charmed by Eduard during their dance lessons, thus contributing to their estrangement or even end of their friendship.

Freud explained that his friend married into money to gain financial independence from his father, who kept him "short enough" (Ibid.) They did meet again, each seeing what the other had become, how life had treated them and the very different directions they had taken. Freud described his friend as someone who was in love with every girl he met, "and now he is with none. I was in love with none and am now with one" (Ibid., p. 98), he commented. Silberstein now wanted to get his drinking buddies together again for an evening, but Freud declined his invitation: he was on duty at the hospital and his thoughts were on other matters.

His account of the end of their friendship creates the impression that despite the permanence of their bond, there was indeed a moment of rupture. Freud justified this by Martha's arrival in his life and the different relationships and goals that ensued. While certainly important, these reasons nevertheless appear secondary; the gap that seems to have deepened between the two friends was likely more closely linked to Freud's renewed attempts at meddling in Eduard's private life, which resulted in the latter's decision to stop the correspondence. Although the end of their relationship was less passionate than their long friendship, it was still a form of breakup. By no longer writing to his faithful correspondent, Eduard put an end to their exchange, while Freud's position on his friend's romantic choices was excessively super-egoic. The episode concerning Eduard's wife Pauline Silberstein and what followed nevertheless shows that they never forgot one another and that the end of their friendship was not marked by intense resentment. The memory of all they had shared as young boys was stronger than their disagreements and differences of opinion. In 1891, Silberstein referred his first wife Pauline, fifteen years younger than him and suffering from depression, to Freud for treatment. While Freud was waiting for her to attend her first session, Pauline committed suicide by jumping from the third floor of his building in Berggasse. Silberstein subsequently had a daughter from his second marriage, who in 1982 visited Anna Freud in London and talked to her about her father's first wife's suicide (Hamilton, 2002).

A last letter was later found, dated 28th April 1910. In it, Freud thanked Eduard for his good wishes and apologised for the delay in responding to his "sign of life". He wanted to hear what had become of his friend and described his own professional situation, scientific achievements and the fact that only his large family prevented him from living a very comfortable life. Eduard had mentioned potential referrals, and Freud answered that they were better to be sent to his pupils, as he was fully booked.

Eduard Silberstein returned to Braila, where he lived until his death in 1925. Despite having obtained a law degree in 1879, he never practiced law but instead supported his family by working at a bank and later in the grain trade. He was actively involved in politics throughout his life and played a role in the affairs of the local Jewish community (De Mijolla, 2002).

In his letter to the Braila B'nai B'rith Lodge, dated 22nd April 1928, Freud said he had been deeply touched by the honours bestowed on Eduard after his death. As time passed by, tensions faded into a much more tender memory. He spoke about their close friendship as a "fraternal fellowship" (Freud, 1871–1881, p. 186), an early bond that "cannot be forgotten". Without specifying the date, Freud wrote he would sometimes see Eduard in Vienna; for a period of time, he was also his physician. He described him as a kind-hearted man with a great sense of humour, which must have certainly made it easier to bear the difficulties of life.

Notes

1 Meaning "away with you".
2 Latin for "the golden age".

3 Veronicas are girls of easy virtue, from the German *Ehrenpreis* (price of honour) denoting the genus *Veronica*.
4 Reading Union for German Students in Vienna.
5 In 1868, Louise Lateau, born in 1850 in Belgium, experienced unexplained stigmata on her feet and her left side. These were accompanied by long periods of ecstasy. After the investigation led by the Belgian Royal Academy of Medicine in 1874, these clinical facts were established as real, which did not prevent one physician, Dr Warlomont, to conclude that Lateau suffered from a neurotic condition.

Chapter 2

Searching for paternal figures

2.1 Summary of a training: Paris and *neurotica*

In the course of his medical studies, Freud had several important encounters. In his first year, in 1871, he attended Karl Claus' lectures on general biology and Darwinism; three years later, he started his career as a researcher at the Institute of Comparative Anatomy directed by Claus. Here he began to focus on the anatomy of eels and received a scholarship to visit, on two occasions, the experimental laboratory in Trieste, at the time an Austrian city which in his comments he nonetheless associated with Italy. During his research, Freud discovered the existence of testicles in male eels. In October 1876, he started as a student researcher at the Vienna Physiological Institute directed by Ernst Brücke, all the while continuing to attend lectures. He became a physician in 1881 and was appointed a demonstrator, and started to gain financial independence, although he was also supported by colleagues or friends such as Josef Breuer.

After Brücke made it clear that there was no future for him in his laboratory, Freud resigned in June 1882, two months after meeting Martha Bernays. He decided to start his own practice and in order to do so undertook various clinical placements in different medical fields. In November 1883, while working in the service of Professor Hermann Nothnagel, he was appointed Aspirant and given a modest salary. In May of the same year, his three-month stay as a researcher in Meynert's psychiatric clinic left a permanent mark on his trajectory. From December 1883 until the summer of 1885, Freud worked in a medical service for nervous and liver diseases directed by Dr Franz Scholz, who was interested in neurology. His wish to specialise in neuropathology emerged as early as 1883 (Bernfeld, 1951).

He was appointed a *Privatdozent* in neuropathology in September 1885 and received another travel grant for a six-month stay abroad. In October he left for Paris to join Charcot's service at the Salpêtrière.

The historians of psychoanalysis have long emphasised the impact of his encounter with Breuer, Charcot and later Bernheim, to follow the trajectory of the elaboration of psychoanalysis. The practice of hypnosis with neurotic patients was indeed the crucible of Freud's fundamental discoveries, which prepared the birth of psychoanalysis. In this theoretical journey, the theory of *Neurotica*, based on the idea

DOI: 10.4324/9781003437062-3

of a child's sexual seduction and its decisive role in adult neurosis, was also key, especially since it enabled Freud to develop, with the case of Emma (1950 [1895]), the idea of retroaction as linking childhood and adolescence. However, in Paris Freud did not just rediscover the effects of hypnosis; he also attended Brouardel's lectures and autopsies at the Paris morgue, which fascinated him. The observations of sexual abuse and violence suffered by children and young people – especially the vaginal and anal rapes that would lead to death – prepared the ground for his future theory of *Neurotica*. As Anzieu explains (1989, p. 523). "Freud's innovation lies in his interest in the psychological consequences for the child and adolescent development and the formation of adult neurosis"; well said indeed, which again attests to the debt which the birth of psychoanalysis owed to Freud's clinical interest in "young people" (Houssier, Christaki, 2016).

2.2   Shameful learning

A number of other events which influenced Freud's work prior to his creation of psychoanalysis also date back to this period. In 1880, Breuer started treating the then-twenty-one-year-old Bertha Pappenheim; her case was later commented on in detail by Freud himself and she was also a friend of Martha. In 1884, Freud saw his first hysteric patient. He took on his first students. In 1886, he opened his private practice, while continuing to work three afternoons per week at the paediatric clinic of Professor Max Kassowitz.

During the ten years between Gisela and Martha, but also between Eduard and Martha, Freud continued to find fault with his father and remained quietly critical of him for not having been a hero. This criticism grew louder when in 1873, after the failure of his first venture in Freiberg, his father, now nearly sixty years old, lost all his capital in the Viennese stock market crash, leaving the family reeling. From now on, Freud's father spent his days strolling around the city and reading; Freud's love of reading drew from his father's own investment in books. However, his father's leniency and lack of ambition also pushed Freud towards stricter father substitutes (Eissler, 1978). His ambivalence set up a contrast between the image of a soft and tender yet weak father and one whose authoritarian demands made him more reliable in terms of making key life decisions. The father as representing authority also offers the possibility of resistance and can eventually undergo a symbolic murder, as any end of adolescence requires.

This period revolved around Freud's professional choices; it was marked by searching for father substitutes, in a series of subsequent displacements. Brücke played a key role in Freud's choice of career; the latter did not fail to render him a tribute when he wrote that he had the most decisive influence in all his life. Brücke had a monolithic personality – the ideal reliable father substitute. An idealised and severe figure, he was indeed what young Freud was unwittingly searching for and the source of several unpleasant memories. Freud wrote about his laboratory years:

> All the dreamer's enjoyment lay in his day-time existence, whereas in his dreams he was still haunted by the shadow of an unhappy life from which he

had at last escaped. Some dreams of my own of a similar kind have enabled me to throw a little light on the subject. As a young doctor I worked for a long time at the Chemical Institute without ever becoming proficient in the skills which that science demands; and for that reason in my waking life I have never liked thinking of this barren and indeed humiliating episode in my apprenticeship. On the other hand I have a regularly recurring dream of working in the laboratory, of carrying out analyses and of having various experiences there. These dreams are disagreeable in the same way as examination dreams and they are never very distinct.

(Freud, 1900, p. 475)

2.3   Becoming someone

Freud (1925) wrote that despite the family's modest circumstances, when it came to his choice of profession, his father encouraged him to follow his own inclinations. In his youth, he felt no special interest for the status and activities of a doctor, but was moved by a curiosity towards more human concerns. Eissler (1978, p. 466) considers that when Freud announces to Emil Fluss that he had decided to become a scientist, in the field of medicine or natural sciences, his tone was rather pessimistic. He mentioned the possibility but did not believe in it, saying that any plan could turn into a "Tower of Babel". His decision was therefore marred by doubts as to his own competence. He seems to have had a bad conscience about his choice of studies, as if wanting to make sure that he does not betray the great intellectual figures of his boyhood, which served him not just in his youth but throughout life. However, Eissler does not take into account the guilt of the idea of failing to become a great man for his mother and the guilt of choosing a path – medicine – which, unlike the Tower of Babel, did not have a potentially grandiose destiny. In this gap lied the challenge of distancing himself from his infantile ideals and, in a way that was painful for Freud, working through his Oedipal desires. The resistance to what had been the basis of his childhood and adolescent position was thus probably not unrelated to his "neurasthenia", linked to his university studies. These conflicts were all the more present for Freud because by leaving behind his adolescent daydreams of grandeur, without nevertheless giving up on them completely, he tried to adjust his ideals to the harsh reality of a researcher. He did not simply "betray" his relationship to his mother, but slowly became the family's main breadwinner and elevated himself beyond the father's own achievements, which he surpassed in all sense of the word. The burden of this responsibility, which now created an evolving barter between the infantile ideal and his position of responsibility in the family, was very difficult to bear.

Medical studies offered a compromise that held incestual fantasies at bay. The "Golden Sigi" might have instead focused on studying politics in order to become a minister. Nevertheless, we can agree with Eissler's distinction between the permissive father when it came to Freud's studies and the inner and more severe father who did not allow Freud to choose freely. Childhood memories associate father with an aggressive and anxiety-provoking figure, even though in reality their relationship seems to have been much less ambivalent. This suggests that, as it is often the case, Freud's inner world during adolescence was greatly more conflictual and repressive than his confrontation with the outer world, with the important exception of his experience of poverty. This idea is connected to his need to create his own path where it was impossible to identify with his father's professional success, in other words an attempt to hold himself, as Winnicott would have put it.

Bernfeld's view (1951) of Freud's professional path is that becoming a doctor required him to turn away from his original interests. As Freud himself wrote (1937), in his youth he had no desire to save suffering humanity. He believed that his innate sadistic tendencies were not very intense and thus he had no need to for this derivative to develop, for example by playing "doctors and patients". His infantile curiosity took other paths. His family felt this lack of interest for medicine, given that he could not stand the sight of blood, as for example during the operation performed on his patient Emma Eckstein (Freud, 1887–1904, p. 117).

Freud's return to his past was subject to multiple reconstructions, as the work of memory generally entails. With regards to his adolescence, we can think of the ambition associated with the megalomanic dreams of teenage years populating Freud's letters to Silberstein (Houssier, 2018a). However, in a letter to Martha he later wrote:

> [I]n the beginning, I wasn't [ambitious]; I was seeking in science the satisfaction which the effort of searching and the moment of discovery offer; I never was one of those people who can't bear the thought of being washed away by death before they have scratched their names on the rock amidst the waves.
>
> (Freud, 1873–1939, p. 57)

In writing those words, he must have forgotten that in case of making a scientific discovery he had wished to keep the "eternal glory of the idea", as I have previously pointed out in one of his letters to Silberstein. He also wrote to Martha that in order to succeed, one must make people talk about oneself, in a less passionate context than what he may have said to Eduard.

This kind of slightly megalomanic daydreaming steeped in his parents' desires continued later in his life, when he wrote to Fliess that he was wondering if one day there would be a plaque on his house indicating that here, the secret of the dream revealed itself to him. These aspirational daydreams, regardless of their later transformation, were an inner support to Freud, at a time when he had to deal with the end of the Spanish Academy, the loss of his friendship with Silberstein, premarital sexual abstinence, poverty and frustrated ambitions. Despite their ongoing conflicts, towards the end of his adolescence and due to his poverty, Freud probably identified more with his father's feelings of failure. At this time, while opening up to new identifications and role models, his first decisive encounter arrived in the laboratory of Professor Brücke, whom Freud later called his "teacher" (Freud, 1900).

2.4 Between ambition and punishment

Joseph Paneth, who alongside Ernst Fleischl repeatedly helped Freud financially, died of tuberculosis in 1890; he was thirty-three years old. He described "Paneth cells", which are part of the intestinal antimicrobial defence. He replaced Freud as Brücke's assistant at the Vienna Physiological Institute, with both of them hoping to be promoted as quickly as possible. Because the turnover turned out to be slow, each of them tended to nurture a few death-wishes towards their various colleagues.

Between 1876 and 1882, Freud's work in Brücke's laboratory was therefore coloured by murderous and rivalrous fantasies:

> There had been a time when I had had to reproach my friend Josef [Paneth] for an attitude of this same kind: 'Ôte-toi que je m'y mette!' He had followed in my footsteps as demonstrator in Brücke's laboratory, but promotion there was slow and tedious. Neither of Brücke's two assistants was inclined to budge from his place, and youth was impatient. My friend, who knew that he could not expect to live long, and whom no bonds of intimacy attached to his immediate superior, sometimes gave loud expression to his impatience.
>
> (Freud, 1900, p. 484)

Paneth's terminal disease became a kind of protection; despite what he said, given his condition nobody could oust him. But the rivalry under Brücke's watchful gaze was not just Paneth's ambition to replace Fleischl:

> Not unnaturally, a few years earlier, I myself had nourished a still livelier wish to fill a vacancy. Wherever there is rank and promotion the way lies open for wishes that call for suppression. Shakespeare's Prince Hal[1] could not, even at his father's sick-bed, resist the temptation of trying on the crown.
>
> (Ibid.)

Freud's ambition was explicitly Oedipal; it was through the symbolic body of his father that he was trying to make a place for himself in the professional world. The remaining associations confirm his identification with Paneth, through the reference to Julius Caesar declaiming that because his rival was ambitious, he slew him. When it came to him, Freud used a cultural metaphor to distance himself from emotions and memories that were still "alive" in him some fifteen years later. Paneth could not wait for Fleischl to cede his position and eventually left the laboratory himself.

The situation echoed somewhat Brücke's later warning to Freud that there was no hope of getting a promotion in his laboratory and he should instead pursue his career elsewhere. However, all devouring ambition had its cost in guilt. Freud associated these murderous challenges for position and power with his own feelings after having attended an unveiling of a memorial at the university. His wish to also have a statue erected in his name required a compensation, which the dream expressed by a simple phrase: "A just punishment! It serves you right!" (Ibid.). The same expression later repeatedly returned in his writing, to reflect of the super-egoic tensions involved.

2.5   No one is unreplaceable

Freud continues his analysis with the series of memories from this period. During Paneth's funeral, a young man made an apparently inopportune comment, suggesting that the orator's words appeared to say that without the deceased, the world would come to an end. The dream-thoughts follow this logic: "It's quite true that no one's irreplaceable. How many people I've followed to the grave already! But I'm still alive. I've survived them all; I'm left in possession of the field." (Ibid, p. 485). These thoughts assailed Freud when he became worried about coming to Berlin and finding his friend Fliess dead – a sign that the honeymoon period of their friendship had come to an end, followed by a strong ambivalence, tainted by his familiar fear – the fantasy of a loved one dying. In his quest for a profession and financial independence, the themes of revenge, punishment and castration were omnipresent, as Freud's analysis of his dreams later revealed.

In a later revision of his book, Freud wrote about the punishment dreams of a parvenu. He compared his situation to that of a journeyman tailor who had grown into a famous author. Implicitly, he described the hopes of a young boy in the midst of a moratorium of study and hard work. The time of waiting for the fulfilment of one's ambitions provoked an "exaggeratedly ambitious phantasy" (Ibid., p. 475), which in the dream was transformed into its opposite. The stifling of ambition and wish-fulfilment led to feelings of humiliation, sketching out one of the key conflicts of Freud's adolescent years. In other words, each time his desires were thwarted, his ambition to become a scientific hero and seduce his mother provoked a feeling of humiliation or shame as to his own value, personal abilities and feelings of impotence. It is therefore no surprise that he linked this dream with masochistic impulses.

Freud's ambitions were also thwarted by a certain slowness in Freud's university trajectory. He returns to this kind of inhibition as follows:

> The manner of my interview with my father in the dream was like an interrogation or examination, and reminded me too of a teacher at the University who used to take down exhaustive particulars from the students who were enrolling themselves for his lectures: "Date of birth?" – "1856". – "*Patre?*" In reply to this, one gave one's father's first name with a Latin termination; and we students assumed that the Hofrat *drew conclusions* from the first name of the father which could not always be drawn from that of the student himself. . . . The interrogation by the professor led to a recollection of the register of University Students (which in my time was drawn up in Latin). It led further to thoughts upon the course of my academic studies.
>
> (Freud, 1900, p. 450)

The habitual period of five years was extended due to Freud's hesitancies and his tendency to spread himself too thin. This led to a feeling of inferiority, the source of his provocative thoughts:

> I quietly went on with my work for several more years; and in my circle of acquaintances I was regarded as an idler and it was doubted whether I should ever get through. Thereupon I *quickly* decided to take my examinations and I got through them *in spite of the delay*. Here was a fresh reinforcement of the dream-thoughts with which I was defiantly confronting my critics: "Even though you won't believe it because I've taken my time, I *shall* get through; I *shall* bring my medical training to a *conclusion*. Things have often turned out like that before."
>
> (Freud, 1900, pp. 450–451)

> There was a very clear reminder in the dream that "*mea res agitur*", in the allusion to Goethe's short but exquisitely written essay; for when at the end of my school-days I was hesitating in my choice of a career, it was hearing that essay read aloud at a public lecture that decided me to take up the study of natural science.
>
> (Ibid., p. 441)

Here, Freud refers to Goethe's text that had been inserted in his bibliography although it has since been attributed to another author. We notice that despite his doubts and sensitivity to potential criticism, Freud seemed solid in his determination.

2.6   Under Brücke's watchful gaze

The following anecdote is one of the best known apropos Freud's time in Brücke's laboratory:

> At the time I have in mind I had been a demonstrator at the Physiological Institute and was due to start work early in the morning. It came to Brücke's ears that I sometimes reached the students' laboratory late. One morning he turned up punctually at the hour of opening and awaited my arrival. His words were brief and to the point. But it was not they that mattered. What overwhelmed me were the terrible blue eyes with which he looked at me and by which I was reduced to nothing. . . . No one who can remember the great man's eyes, which retained their striking beauty even in his old age, and who has ever seen him in anger, will find it difficult to picture the young sinner's emotions.
>
> (Ibid., p. 422)

Freud added that thanks to Brücke's energetic intervention, he never again let a discovery go without a publication, putting an end to his young researcher's dilettantism and procrastination.

Freud's laboratory duties essentially consisted in working with the microscope. The Cretaceous fish returned on multiple occasions. First, Freud mentioned a book on the nervous system of fish by "Stannius", an author he greatly admired. He added that the first research entrusted to him by his teacher was to study the nervous system of the *ammocoete*.

While previously marvelling at the works of Virgil, Sophocles and Goethe, Freud now had to restrict his interests to the static visual field (the microscope), forcing him to repress his fantasies and letting his imaginative powers lay fallow. However, Freud's work during this time shows that he was able to transform dead images into something highly dynamic (Eissler, 1978). Breger (2000) suggests another, complementary perspective: microscopic research was a kind of training in scientific asceticism and denial.

During his years of training, while working for Nothnagel, Freud made an original observation when he identified the role of the spinal ganglion cells in the evolutionary transition (Freud, 1877). Eissler interprets this kind of creativity as using scientific interpretation of visual structures by following strict rules of reason and rationality, which protected Freud against transgressive impulses. At the same time, the proximity of the microscope also offered great satisfaction of seeing something new and identifying it as such.

Breger (2000) highlights that Brücke was not only a scientist and rationalist but also a lover of painting, who saw himself as a cultural ambassador to his students. Freud was drawn to his personality split between science and culture; we do not know whether he was aware that his teacher had also lost a son.

Freud later wrote to his fiancée that his years at Brücke's laboratory were some of his best times as a student, when he was free of any other desires. We might assume that this is a slightly idealising reconstruction. It is true that at the time, he had found a libidinal refuge in pursuing a scientific goal while guided by and identified with his teacher. However, as Eissler points out, working for Brücke also freed him from his forbidden sexual desires, shoring up his defences, while he remained psychically available for his encounter with Martha. Freud himself described the feelings of satisfaction at being able to meet people he respected and regarded as role models: Brücke, but also his assistants Exner and especially Ernst von Fleischl-Marxow, who became a close friend.

It was still during his time at the Physiological Institute that Freud met Breuer, another figure of paternal identification (Bernfeld, 1944). During his two trips to Trieste in 1876, he closely studied the testicles of some four hundred eels. The explosive alliance between experimental science and sexuality – a fitting subject for the future creator of psychoanalysis.

2.7   On eels and women

Freud visited Trieste on a scholarship; he was dismayed by the local women, whose fashion habits reminded him of the "more dubious classes of society". The women he saw were identified with cats; he protected himself from them by regarding them as untouchable, while others were too ugly to interest him. "He interiorised the constraints of his education to such a degree that he could only react defensively, and naturally also by renouncing his drives," Boelich points out (1990, p. 26).

Two weeks later, during a trip to the small fishing village of Muccia, women seemed much more attractive than in Trieste. And yet, midwives and pregnant women provoke a certain feeling of avoidance, "because the consequences were so visible" (Idem). In a region where women seemed so fertile to Freud, while he was involved in his research on eel reproduction, "the punishment for possession is the shame of pregnancy". This echoes what he later wrote to Martha, after seeing a performance of *Carmen*, namely that the mob gave in to its appetites, while the two of them deprived themselves (Freud, 1873–1939, p. 50).

Gallo (2009) sees the journey to Trieste as a key moment in Freud's commitment to science, which established a mode of psychic functioning that sublimated sexual conflicts through research. In studying the genitals of eels, Freud tackled the enigma of reproduction, of origins, as well as the bisexuality of eels. "In complete contrast to the diffuse character of my studies during my earlier years at the University, I was now developing an inclination to concentrate my work exclusively upon a single subject or problem" (Freud, 1925, p. 11).

His three letters to Eduard written during his first semester in Trieste in 1876 constitute a key source of information on this period in Freud's life. Let's return to them. In the first letter, Freud gave Eduard his address. He alluded to the beauty of the town and its inhabitants but said he would prefer to give him the details in person. He had also been swimming (Bernfeld, 1951). On 5th April he spoke about his wish to go to the theatre, specifically to see Shakespeare's *Othello*. This letter, the only one to contain Freud's illustrations, was mostly devoted to his research and "the great problems connected with the words ducts, testicles, and ovaries, world-renowned words" (Freud, 1871–1881, p. 142). Even though he described Italian men and women, he wrote that because the dissection of human beings was not allowed, "I really have nothing to do with them" (p. 145).

The letter of 25th April speaks about his changing attitude to letter writing. After he had already freed himself of his desire to answer letters, the wish returned, and he explained to Eduard that his mood had seen a "complete transformation" (p. 150). This was due to his inability to "stick to any place or subject to the bitter end", his impatience. He mentioned the city's history and his way of life there, as well as a walk in Muccia, where he saw that two of the landladies of different pubs were pregnant. Following Brentano's probability computations, this raised the expectations of other landladies even higher. His jokes about prostitutes or pregnant women resonate with an infantile sexual theory: do these women bear fruit the whole year round or only at certain times and all together, he asks. Sexual activity appeared here as an excess; women's sexuality was transgressive. The town's beautiful girls and children were distinguished from the ugly women of Trieste, even though their class of population "ought by rights to be beautiful" (p. 153). However, Freud returned to his first day in Trieste, when he felt that the city was full of "Italian goddesses, and I was filled with apprehension". The next day, full of expectations, fear and fascination, he was disappointed not to see any more of these. He also announced that he would return to Trieste, from 2nd September to 1st October 1876.

Writing to Knöpfmacher on 6th August 1878, Freud explained that he had moved to a different laboratory to pursue his "real profession: 'flaying of animals or torturing of human beings'", jokingly adding that he preferred the latter. The quotation comes from the preface to *Max and Moritz*, by Wilhelm Busch; it in fact reads: "*teasing* human beings and *torturing* animals" (1865, p., Houssier, 2013, my emphasis). Reversing the formula changes little: in the story Freud was referring to, the two heroes, rascals resembling two teenage boys, are eventually killed by humans and eaten by animals. This raises the question of whether Freud was really so free of infantile sadism as he later suggested when speaking of the origins of his professional career (Freud, 1925). Later, he wrote to Martha that when he was bored, he would sometimes torment the two rabbits who came to look for food in his room and would make a mess on the floor (Freud, 1873–1939, p. 140).

At the end of this period, Freud's primary interest among the medical specialities was Meynert's psychiatry. He was not convinced he would become a doctor and was not more interested in physiological and histological research. From May 1881 to June 1882, he worked as Brücke's teaching assistant. When he thus dropped his eel study, which was connected to Brücke, and turned his interest towards Flechsig's psychiatric work including new methods of study, Brücke felt betrayed. His distancing was interpreted by Freud as a sign of jealousy and hostility rather than an interest in Flechsig's work praised by Freud in his first articles. This undermined his loyalty to Brücke and provoked intense feelings of guilt (Bernfeld, 1951). The dream he described to his fiancée was probably an illustration of punishment dreams: in it, Brücke was telling him that he had little hope getting a scholarship, because each of the seven other candidates was in a better position than him.

2.8   The last advice. Two images of the father

In his letter to Eduard dated 22nd July 1879, he first spoke about a physiology examination during which Brücke was in a bad mood and did not give him the chance to shine (Freud, 1871–1881, p. 171). As a good student, he was asked to examine the microscope, which were smaller matters than what he thought he would be given and where he could show off his knowledge. Nevertheless, he finished ahead of the others, of whom one student failed, which annoyed Brücke, who did not want others to see that Freud was doing something different after he had finished. Fleischl told him the next day that Brücke asked him to test Freud, and Fleischl said that Freud would probably know everything. Freud assumed that had he asked Fleischl for the questions beforehand, he would have gotten them. "Which goes to show that it pays to be brazen, and I shall be so from now on" (p. 171).

In his first *rigorosum*, which included questions from biology, chemistry and botany, he got an "excellent" distinction, even though he said he was able to avoid disaster only thanks to the kindness of fate or his examiner, his friend Fleischl. In the second *rigorosum*, on general medicine, he was only passed as "satisfactory", because he failed forensic medicine. The third *rigorosum* followed ten months later and covered various medical specialities; here too Freud received an "excellent", especially thanks to his photographic memory.

His graduation ceremony in 1881 was attended by his childhood friends from Freiberg, his family and Richard Fluss, Gisela and Emil's brother. A turning point came in 1882, "when my teacher, for whom I felt the highest possible esteem, corrected my father's generous improvidence" (Freud, 1925, p. 10) and urged him to leave his laboratory. Why did Freud let himself be swayed by this non-choice and, as a result, lose three years of his studies? There were a number of things at stake: despite his father's financial woes, the latter continued to support him without reservations, leaving him complete freedom in his decisions. It seems that Jacob was concerned by his son's chaotic first few years at university; instead of five, Freud took eight years to earn his degree. Jacob was preparing his marriage with his Manchester niece Pauline, which Freud rejected without any regrets, contrary to his loss of Gisela. He also thought of introducing his son into the business world. He was proud of Freud, who continued his histological studies instead of trying to earn a living as a doctor; he put no pressure on him to enter the sphere of work.

However, when Brücke took a position opposing the flexible but arguably "liberal" attitude of Freud's father by advising Freud to give up theoretical studies due to his difficult material situation, Freud did a one-eighty. Brücke positioned himself as a more realistic father, using his authority to intervene in the highly charged relationship between Freud and his father. Sigmund took his advice and in 1882 left the physiology laboratory to join the General Hospital as a clinical assistant. During his work across the different hospital services, he focused primarily on obtaining experience that would allow him to open his own practice. This time, there was no longer any question of delaying his adult life by keeping his libidinal status quo. The faraway prospect of success became a realistic project supported by a "heavy" paternal figure which functioned as a third party in Freud's inner conflicts. The latter revolved around a central conflict between maintaining a bisexual incestual cathexis, which meant delaying his studies by remaining closer to his family, and the Oedipal voice represented by Brücke, which basically communicated to him that it was now time to concretise his professional plans instead of waiting for a fictional place in his laboratory. He told Freud clearly that the place was already taken, and he would not let go of his assistant. Freud's family situation and his relationship with Martha also forced him to leave. His fiancée was of modest means, which Freud was explicitly proud of, and his promotion to full professorship was uncertain; he would have been unable to support a family, neither his own nor the one he wanted to start with his fiancée. He therefore decided to knock at the door or the hospital's Chair, Professor Hermann Nothnagel.

2.9 A short conversation with Nothnagel

When he confided in Martha, Freud spoke openly about his visit to Nothnagel, whom he tried to convince to take him on. He described his unease before "a man

who has so much power over us, and over whom we have none". He felt shaky outside, but more assured once inside, "as usual in battle" (Freud, 1873–1939, p. 31).
He came with a recommendation from Meynert to be taken on as an assistant and
asked for the position of Aspirant with Nothnagel rather than at the General Hospital. When Nothnagel said that he would keep him in mind, Freud argued he needed
to finish his studies as quickly as possible "in order to set myself up in practice",
probably near his relatives in England.

In Freud's account of the conversation, Nothnagel asked him which career he
would choose – academic or practical? Freud answered that "my inclinations and
my past experience" pointed toward the former, but he needed to live and earn his
living. But no matter – Nothnagel's response was essentially: we shall see. Freud
thought of becoming a dermatologist for a wealthy clientele. Earning a living now
became a definitive goal, beyond the long nurtured Oedipal promise of becoming a
rich "Golden Sigi". Given his father's inability to provide his family with relative
material comfort, the hard laws of necessity now weighted solely on Freud.

In his dream book, Freud returned to his father's failure to support the family in
the following terms:

> [It] occurred after I had heard that a senior colleague of mine, whose judgement
> was regarded as beyond criticism, had given voice to disapproval and surprise
> at the fact that the psychoanalytic treatment of one of my patients had already
> entered its *fifth year*. The first sentences of the dream alluded under a transparent
> disguise to the fact that for some time this colleague had taken over the duties
> which my father could no longer fulfil ("*fees due*", "*maintenance in the hospi-
> tal*"), and that, when our relations began to be less friendly, I became involved
> in the same kind of emotional conflict which, when a misunderstanding arises
> between a father and son, is inevitably produced.
>
> (p. 437)

The colleague in question is probably Breuer, who before their disagreement
had initially provided material support. Freud continued with dream-thoughts
that could well have applied to himself, when he complained of his neurasthenia,
underpinned by guilt:

> The dream-thoughts protested bitterly against the reproach that I was *not get-
> ting on faster* – a reproach which, applying first to my treatment of the patient,
> extended later to other things. Did he know anyone, I thought, who could get
> on more quickly? Was he not aware that, apart from my methods of treat-
> ment, conditions of that kind are altogether incurable and last a life-time? What
> were *four or five years* in comparison with a whole life-time, especially con-
> sidering that the patient's existence had been so very much eased during the
> treatment?
>
> (Freud, 1900, pp. 436–437)

In July 1882, Freud finally became an Aspirant at Nothnagel's clinic. He was revolted by the poor quality of care: patients had no lights, with ten cases of tuberculosis crammed in a dusty room of twenty. Did these patients "not have a right . . . to a larger share of what society has deprived them of due to its bad organization, by no fault of their own", he writes to Martha in February 1884, comparing the costs of improving these patients' quality of life with the "vain equipping of our European armies". Because there was no future for him at the Physiological Institute, he was hoping to become financially independent in 1882–1885, and spent three years at the Vienna General Hospital, while also beginning to experiment, in 1884, with cocaine – on himself and some of his close friends.

Nothnagel may have appeared cold towards Freud, but he also suggested to him the idea of using electrotherapy on his patients; he saw it as potentially a lucrative market. Freud thus hoped to be sent patients for this type of treatment; he later wrote that he abandoned the method due to its complete inefficacy (Freud, 1910a). Once again, he distanced himself from a "teacher" he had at first admired. The repetition of this ambivalence towards his teachers leaves little doubt as to Freud's inner conflicts, which he later described in the analyses of his dreams. However, the connection between the two men was never completely broken off. In 1902, Nothnagel in fact recommended to Freud the psychiatrist Paul Federn, who wished to meet him after having read the *Interpretation of Dreams*. Federn soon became part of the original Wednesday Society as its fourth member and no doubt one of the most influential people in the psychoanalytic movement (Houssier et al., 2017).

2.10   Meynert and male hysteria

During his time at the Vienna General Hospital, where he was soon promoted, Freud worked in various services, including spending a semester with Thomas Meynert, a professor of psychiatry he had greatly admired as a student, both for his work and his personality. As a researcher at the Institute of Cerebral Anatomy, Meynert now asked him to focus exclusively on brain anatomy. Meynert was a brain anatomist and a professor of psychiatry; Freud later said that he followed faithfully in his tracks. In 1882, his appointment as a Privat-Dozent was confirmed by the Ministry. A memory of this appointment appears in the dream of the botanical monograph:

> From that point my thoughts must have gone back to the beginning of my career as University Lecturer when I in fact had no lecture room and when my efforts to get hold of one met with little response from the powerfully placed Hofrats and Professors. In those circumstances I had gone to L., who at that time held the office of Dean of the Faculty and who I believed was friendlily disposed to me, to complain of my troubles. He promised to help me, but I heard nothing more from him. In the dream he was Archimedes, giving me a ποῦ στῶ [footing] and himself leading me to the new locality. Anyone who is an adept

at interpretation will guess that the dream-thoughts were not exactly free from ideas of vengeance and self-importance. It seems clear, in any case, that without this exciting cause Archimedes would scarcely have found his way into my dream that night.

(Freud, 1900, p. 168)

Learning about the organic pathologies of the brain, Freud gained renown for his diagnostic abilities, such as diagnosing the first case of polyneuritis acuta (1925, p. 12). He lectured to American physicians but did not understand anything about the neuroses. When he presented a case of a persistent headache as a case of meningitis, the audience was revolted and his activities as a teacher came to an end. However, at this time, "greater authorities than myself in Vienna were in the habit of diagnosing neurasthenia as a cerebral tumour" (p. 12).

Freud initially admired Meynert's genius, before their relationship cooled off. He became an assistant in Meynert's psychiatric clinic and was also given a heated room as well as a decent salary (Bernfeld, 1951). In one of his letters to Martha, he wrote about an incident with one of Meynert's colleagues, Pfungen, whose supposedly eccentric and delusional ideas he contradicted in front of Meynert. In connection with this "friction", he confided in his fiancée that he too can see a tyrannical streak in his own nature and finds it difficult to submit (Freud, 1873–1939, p. 52).

His dreams provide more material, as well as the following story:

Here the figure for whom he stood was no less a person than the great Meynert, in whose footsteps I had trodden with such deep veneration and whose behaviour towards me, after a short period of favour, had turned to undisguised hostility. The dream reminded me that he himself had told me that at one time in his youth he had indulged in the habit of making himself *intoxicated with chloroform* and that on account of it he had had to go into a *home*. It also reminded me of another incident with him shortly before his death. I had carried on an embittered controversy with him in writing, on the subject of male hysteria, the existence of which he denied. When I visited him during his fatal illness and asked after his condition, he spoke at some length about his state and ended with these words: "You know, I was always one of the clearest cases of male hysteria." He was thus admitting, to my satisfaction and astonishment, what he had for so long obstinately contested.

(Freud, 1900, pp. 437–438)

Freud fills in a direct connection with his father, who is here again criticised as to his professional status:

But the reason why I was able in this scene of the dream to use my father as a screen for Meynert did not lie in any analogy that I had discovered between the two figures. The scene was a concise but entirely adequate representation of a conditional sentence in the dream-thoughts, which ran in full: "If only I had been the second generation, the son of a professor or Hofrat,[2] I should certainly have *got on faster*."

(Ibid.)

Freud turns his family romance – imagining a powerful and accomplished father who would protect him and possibly inspire him – into a source of rivalrous tension with Meynert.

He later wrote about Meynert: "[He] promised to hand over his lecturing work to me, as he felt he was too old to manage the newer methods. This I declined, in alarm at the magnitude of the task", as well as having had an inkling that this great man was not entirely kindly disposed towards him (Freud, 1925, p. 11). Freud studied nervous diseases, of which there were few specialists in Vienna at the time. The material was therefore dispersed across different services and there was no training available. "One was forced to be one's own teacher", Freud adds, his last comment not without an echo of his reproach to his father – leaving him alone rather than helping him resolve his neurotic conflicts through a voice of authority. Or indeed to guide him, rather than leaving him to his fantasies of self-engendering, as the idea of being one's teacher suggests.

2.11 Early work with children and young people

Dr Kassowitz, professor of paediatrics and the head of a public institute for the treatment of children's diseases in Vienna, wanted to make his institution a children's polyclinic, the first of its kind, and put Freud in charge of a department for the nervous diseases, as Freud wrote to his fiancée in July 1885 (Freud, 1873–1939). In a letter from February 1886, he then described his work in detail: together with a student or two, he carried out consultations in a special room, twice or three times weekly. These were free of charge. He indicated that in return he had the clinical material and, given his status as a Dozent, it could be turned into lectures. He was mostly interested in having access to these cases and the reputation he could acquire as a specialist. He was able to speak to patients, examine them under supervision, but not treat them. In his book on dreams, he alludes to his time at the polyclinic as follows:

> My friend Leopold was also a physician and a relative of Otto's.[3] Since they both specialized in the same branch of medicine, it was their fate to be in competition with each other, and comparisons were constantly being drawn between them. Both of them acted as my assistants for years while I was still in charge of the neurological out-patients' department of a children's hospital. Scenes such as the one represented in the dream used often to occur there. While I was discussing the diagnosis of a case with Otto, Leopold would be examining the child once more and would make an unexpected contribution to our decision.

(Freud, 1900, p. 112)

He was greatly touched by the children at the clinic and preferred them to adults; he speaks about how "touching" the little creatures were when they suffer. "I think I would find my way about in a children's practice in no time" (Freud, 1873–1939, p. 212). From 1886 to 1897, Freud was in charge of the neurology service. He wrote a number of articles on child neurology and is thus often considered the founder of neuropaediatrics. On 25th April 1886, he opened his own practice. Interestingly, in the Sigmund Freud archives at the Library of Congress in Washington, the references pertaining to this period suggest that Freud's consultations at the polyclinic also included adolescent patients. The work of the 4th division of the clinic was the subject of three articles published between 1884 and 1886, which included a great deal of neurological deduction (Bernfeld, 1951). Among the cases studied in these articles from Freud's neurological period, there was a case of a sixteen-year-old cobbler's apprentice who suffered from bleeding gums and small haemorrhages in the lower limbs. Another text mentioned the unpublished case of a young baker with endocarditis.

In 1885, Freud defended his thesis in neuropathology and became Privat-Dozent,[4] with the right to lecture at the university. His examination jury included Brücke, Meynert and Nothnagel, the three great figures that marked his professional beginnings.

He was given a teaching post with a limited number of courses (one or two classes of one to two hours) in the medical field. He obtained this position in June 1885 after having presented in front of Brücke, Meynert, Fleischl, several Privatdozents, assistants, physicians and many students. His dissertation on neuropathology was entitled "The Medullary Tracts of the Brain" and was based on his histological and clinical work; he was accepted unanimously and confirmed, in September, by the Ministry of Public Education – after three years at the General Hospital and nine years of university studies.

Having thus secured his teaching load, Freud then started working on another project: a study stay in Paris, where Charcot's name already exerted a powerful force of attraction. In June, on Breuer's recommendation, he received a travel grant, which funded his medical research in Paris from October 1885 to February 1886.

2.12   A rescue fantasy in Paris

I will not cover all of the aspects of Freud's time in Paris, where he stayed in the Hotel du Brésil[5] in the sixteenth arrondissement and instead focussed on what is more closely connected to the problem of adolescence. In the poverty and austerity of Freud's youth, travel was a forbidden luxury, because his father could not afford such amusements. The journey was also a repetition, of once again being separated from the person he loved: after Eduard, the situation now repeated with Martha, as we shall later discuss, leading to another epistolary relationship. Shortly after arriving in Paris, now aged twenty-eight, Freud felt a strong wish to be helped and protected. As he was walking through the city streets, he concocted the following fantasy: he saw himself before a horse that has bolted, ordering it to stop. A famous person alighted from the carriage and said to him: "You're my saviour, I owe my life to you. What can I do for you?" The wish to be rescued thus turned into its opposite; Freud later realised that he had likely read a similar scene in a story by Franz Hoffmann when he was between eleven and thirteen years old (Trosman, 1969).

He concluded that the part of him resisting the memory of this fantasy and its origins tried to refuse his father's protection. He interpreted this impulse as a struggle against the feeling of dependency on his father and his protective favour. Freud (1901b) later referred a deeper meaning of this fantasy to Karl Abraham's 1922 article on rescue fantasies.

Let us look at this reference more closely. Abraham first cited Freud's works on the psychology of love and specifically the object-choice in men; he then argued that rescue fantasies were linked to fantasies of saving one's father or mother. The son's tender feelings for the mother went hand in hand with a wish to give her a child. The son also saved his father's life in order not to take it from him; rescuing father was the submerged part of the unconscious desire to kill him. Saving the father also meant being "quits" with him: each side now owed their life to the other. This kind of annulment of the generational difference was not unrelated to the fantasy of self-engendering. The rescuing revealed a parricidal tendency but also the desire to separate the parents, as well as to castrate the father and his previously admired virility. For Abraham, this parricidal defiance was a typical neurotic fantasy harking back to the Oedipal myth, whereby "the son's conflict with the father [in adolescence] is transplanted to the earliest past" (Abraham, 1922, p. 472). Abraham was probably the first psychoanalyst to link the Oedipal parricide to the central symbolic conflict of the process of adolescence. The son had to confront his father to find his own path in life and actually be (re)born, which resonated strongly with Freud's own trajectory throughout his studies and beyond. Oedipus' journey to Thebes was a second representation of his birth, Abraham added. Helping others, which after all was what Freud dedicated his life to, was thus a typically adolescent rescue fantasy, underpinned by acute Oedipal guilt.

2.13   Doing without father's sexual permission

Death fantasies were implicit in Freud's discourse about Paris, which we could link to the period of working through his parricidal wishes and dreams of grandeur:

> I was delighted because I had once more survived someone. . . . I was delighted to survive, and I gave expression to my delight with all the naive egoism shown in the anecdote of the married couple one of whom said to the other: "If one of us dies, I shall move to Paris." So obvious was it to me that I should not be the one to die. . . . Thus it seemed to me quite natural that the *revenants* should only exist for just so long as one likes and should be removable at a wish. We have seen what my friend Josef was punished for. . . . It was in that way that Gulliver extinguished the great fire in Lilliput. . . . But Gargantua, too, Rabelais'

superman, revenged himself in the same way on the Parisians by sitting astride on Notre Dame and turning his stream of urine upon the city. It was only on the previous evening before going to sleep that I had been turning over Garnier's illustrations to Rabelais. And, strangely enough, here was another piece of evidence that I was the superman. The platform of Notre Dame was my favourite resort in Paris; every free afternoon I used to clamber about there on the towers of the church between the monsters and the devils. The fact that all the faeces disappeared so quickly under the stream recalled the motto: "*Afflavit et dissipati sunt*", which I intended one day to put at the head of a chapter upon the therapy of hysteria.

(Freud, 1900, pp. 469, 485)

He wrote to Martha that he would return from his journey triumphant, surrounded by an enormous halo, that they would get married and that he would cure all the incurable nervous cases. In his enthusiasm, he wanted to kiss her till she was strong and gay and happy – and "if they haven't died, they are still alive today", a traditional ending of German fairy tales. However, the reality he found on his return was quite different. In October 1886, he spoke before the Medical Society on male hysteria, drawing on Charcot's theories. The response of his colleagues was completely dismissive and Freud's hopes of using hypnosis as a therapeutic technique forced him to return to France in 1889, this time to Bernheim's clinic in Nancy (Eissler, 2006).

His hopes of becoming a psychiatric superman, a hero, involved a fantasy experienced as transgressive: a wish to do without his father's permission, to cease searching for always the same identificatory models. Simply put, one of the signs of working through his parricidal fantasies was the idea of self-authorisation, at a time when it was expected to ask for parental consent to marry. Before starting his relationship with Martha, which represented another period of working through his sexuality and probably marking the end of his adolescence, he described this transition as follows:

A great part of the impression of absurdity in this dream was brought about by running together sentences from different parts of the dream-thoughts without any transition. Thus the sentence "*I went to him in the next room*", etc., dropped the subject with which the preceding sentences had been dealing and correctly reproduced the circumstances in which I informed my father of my having become engaged to be married without consulting him. This sentence was therefore reminding me of the admirable unselfishness displayed by the old man on that occasion, and contrasting it with the behaviour of someone else – of yet another person. It is to be observed that the dream was allowed to ridicule my father because in the dream-thoughts he was held up in unqualified admiration as a model to other people.

(Freud, 1900, p. 437)

With Martha, Freud again felt the pain of separation from a loved one:

The most blatant and disturbing absurdity in the dream resides in its treatment of the date 1851, which seemed to me not to differ from 1856, *just as though a difference of five years was of no significance whatever*. But this last was precisely what the dream-thoughts sought to express. *Four or five years* was the length of time during which I enjoyed the support of the colleague whom I mentioned earlier in this analysis; but it was also the length of time during which I made my *fiancée* wait for our marriage; and it was also, by a chance coincidence which was eagerly exploited by the dream-thoughts, the length of time during which I made my patient of longest standing wait for a complete recovery. '*What are five years?*' asked the dream-thoughts.

(Freud, 1900, p. 438)

Another example of these ambivalent identifications with male figures was pointed out by Eissler with regards to Breuer (Eissler, 1978). First, note Breuer's influence on Freud when the latter called his fiancée "Cordelia" – this was also Breuer's nickname for his wife (Freud, 1873–1939, p. 40); he later named his daughter Mathilde, Frau Breuer's given name. In Shakespeare's *King Lear*, Cordelia cannot show affection for anyone but her husband, not even for her father. Eissler points out that Breuer spoke to Freud about the case of Anna O already in November 1882; we find a trace of this in one of Freud's letters to Martha, when he wrote that he and Breuer discussed "strange case histories – your friend Bertha Pappenheim" (Freud, 1873–1939, p. 41).

Freud in general associated his discovery of hypnosis with his time at Charcot's clinic, beginning in 1885. Eissler argues that given the time it took for this interest to mature in Freud, he could not have manifested it during his discussions with Breuer, even after his first period in Paris. It was only in 1889 that Freud began to seriously consider the kind of treatment Breuer was proposing.

When he returned to this moment in his autobiographical study (Freud, 1925, p. 16), he critiqued Erb and his electrotherapy as "the construction of phantasy" which had "no more relation to reality than some 'Egyptian' dream-book". This experience was "painful, but it helped to rid me of another shred of the innocent faith in authority from which I was not yet free" (Ibid). As a student, he attended a performance by the magnetist Hansen; he noticed that one of the experimental subjects had become deathly pale and fell into a cataleptic stupor, remaining thus for as long as the condition lasted. "This firmly convinced me of the genuineness of the phenomena of hypnosis," he concluded, relegating the figures of Breuer and Charcot to the background.

However, the fact remains that in the mid-1880s, these two figures remained opposed to each other: the idealised image of Charcot versus the more ambivalent Breuer. While Freud's ambivalence in his relationship to father remained unchanged, his meeting with Martha was probably a decisive moment for more than one reason, triggering great many dysthymic oscillations to eventually find a calmer way forward.

Notes

1 Prince Henry, the future Henry V.
2 Court councillor.
3 This would be Oscar Rie, a paediatrician, Freud's assistant at Kassowitz's children's clinic.
4 A university lecturer who has completed a *habilitation* but has not been given a permanent post. A Privatdozent therefore received no salary, but the position was a necessary step to academic advancement. In addition to private tuition, a Privatdozent was also allowed to give university lectures.
5 Today, a plaque on the wall of the hotel still commemorates his stay.

Chapter 3

Martha

Changing the love-object

In relation to Freud's correspondence with his fiancée Martha Bernays, I have already highlighted his still largely adolescent position at the time of their first meeting in April 1882 (Houssier, 2018a). She was then twenty-one; he was twenty-six.

They quickly became engaged and married in 1886, thanks to the generosity of one of Martha's aunts. To Freud's great chagrin, after the death of Martha's father in 1878, her mother moved with her daughters to Wandsbek near Hamburg. This meant a more than four-year separation for the two lovers, resulting in Freud's most prolific correspondence, which includes many reflections on his not yet finished adolescence. He wrote to her enthusiastically: "Why didn't I become a gardener instead of a doctor or writer?" (Freud, 1873–1939, p. 40). Being a gardener had to do with Martha's stay at the gardener's house in the village of Dusternbrook. His words communicate his burning desire to see her again – a passion previously seen in his letters to Eduard – but also highlight his double commitment to medicine and writing. It is unlikely that he had never dreamt of becoming a writer, given his identifications with Goethe and Shakespeare or his intense love of books. In an interview by Papini (1973), Freud stated:

> It's a terrible mistake to think I derive my scientific personality from my work. . . . In reality, I am by nature an artist. . . . I would have loved to have been a poet and throughout my life I wanted to write novels, etc.

Wittels (1924) also mentions a conversation with Stekel, in whom Freud apparently confided that he wanted to become a novelist (Eissler, 1978). Again, we find a clear trace of this wish in the "little novel" included in his letters to Silberstein.

As in the case of Freud's correspondence with his friend, I would like to first give an overview of the contents of his courtship letters with respect to the material related to his adolescence, before diving directly into their exchanges.

3.1   An overview: from exaltation to tranquillity

Grubrich-Simitis and Lortholary (2012) provide an account of the entire four-year period of this correspondence, which includes Martha's as well as Freud's writing.

DOI: 10.4324/9781003437062-4

Based on their synthesis, we could argue that Freud's meeting with Martha offers different ways of looking at the psychic movements linked to a potential end of adolescence, which should be seen as a partial albeit decisive process, rather than a distinct endpoint.

In German, their correspondence makes up five volumes, each given a quote as a title. To only mention two, the first volume is called: "Be Mine as I Imagine You", and the third one "Waiting Quietly and with Surrender, Waiting Struggling and with Exasperation". The titles express Freud's double psychic work, a shift from auto-erotic daydreaming to facing reality, the most significant effects of which we have already explored in terms of his search for paternal substitutes. Ten years after the fantasies sparked off by the *coup de foudre* with Gisela and her mother, this transition involved both an encounter with a "real" object and a movement of opening oneself to otherness, which is a key part of adolescence and includes the integration of one's own femininity. Between these two periods, the variations and connections between receptive passivity and sometimes defensive activity, seen in the opposition between "surrender" and "struggle", mark the intensity of Freud's conflict when again separated from the object of his affection.

The beginning of their love story was highly conflictual and Freud repeatedly experienced feelings of intense jealousy and suspicion. Although some of the letters, published in French by E. Freud (1873–1939), are sometimes highly eloquent in this sense, they tell us little about their protagonists' "sentimental education" or the nature of these first disagreements. "This choice also largely obscures the vulnerability of Freud's relative adolescence, as well as the surprising perspicacity and independence of the even younger Martha," the authors point out (Grubrich-Simitis, Lortholary, 2012, p. 780). They also highlight the lovers' intellectual collaboration, especially Martha's critical mind. After Freud's attempt at finding a double in Eduard, this new bond also provided a form of completeness to his hunger for intellectual debate, of which the previously explored image of Eleanora Fluss could be seen as a kind of harbinger.

When they first met, Freud was an Aspirant in the psychiatric service of the Vienna General Hospital, "planning to dissect a new-born's brain" (Ibid., p. 781). He described to Martha his experiences in the laboratory as a neurologist working on the microscopic anatomy of the brain, testing his measuring tools such as the dynamometer to determine muscular energy and experiment on himself and different animals: frogs, cats or rabbits, after having previously studied eels.

In their letters it was Martha who first mentioned unconscious psychic life, though the term "unconscious" had already appeared in Freud's letters to Silberstein. After a period of silence, she wondered if she had not unconsciously hurt his feelings (Ibid. p. 785). Later in 1883, she realised she identified with him, writing that she had unconsciously taken on his idiosyncrasies, such as his writing style or his way of discussing things.

Shortly after their secret engagement on 17th June 1882, Martha left with her mother and sister Minna. On returning from a visit to Wandsbek, Freud's letters sounded an aggressive tone, after which he worried that she might be cross with him. He excused himself and said he had only opened his suffering heart to her in order to share his feelings.

Martha's personality shines through these letters as well. For example, she was sensitive to her fiancée's fragility and wrote that he should count himself lucky that she was not as strange as him. She appears intuitive, poised, tactful, human, a keen and subtle observer; she lays down clear rules in reality, specifically not to trigger Freud's suspiciousness. She quickly understood her fiancé's situation: due to his poverty and because of his wish to start a family, he wanted to succeed as a scientist, to become famous in order to provide for their future. Hence his tendency to both overwork himself and spend time in his fantasy world.

Likewise, she never tried to normalise the eccentric man she had fallen in love with, although at times she was not shy to put her foot down and sort out various practical issues (visits, debts to be paid, social obligations and so on). Freud recognised this very early on. In November 1882, he wrote: "[H]old my hand firmly on the path we are on together. Even though I might like I'm guiding you, it is in fact you who are my support and my guiding angel" (Ibid., p. 789). A young man bursting with energy and ideas, Freud was overwhelmed by his trials and tribulations, prone to violent mood swings; he was touchy and sometimes harsh towards his loved ones. The poverty of his youth had given him a taste of hunger and contributed to his lasting ambivalence towards his father, who had held his hand on their forest walks.

Because he had not yet learnt to know himself, Freud repeatedly gave in to severe fits of mistrust, which plagued their relationship. He would become demanding and angry, and then return repentant and ashamed, blaming his behaviour on "excessive touchiness and bad temper". On 8th August 1882, after yet another fit of jealousy, he wrote to his beloved: "I think my imagination is somewhat sick and plays dirty tricks on me. It constantly brings various scenes into my mind. . . . A sick person should be taken care of and treated with kindness." These imaginary scenes, especially scenarios of his fiancée being seduced by another man, stemmed from his jealousy, the sources of which, he later wrote, were strongly linked to homosexual fantasies. Only towards the end of their courtship did Freud become truly aware of his melancholia and depressive tendencies, as well as the psychosomatic nature of his various physical ailments (headaches, stomach-aches, fatigue).

In these circumstances, he often felt the need to numb himself. On 17th January 1884, he wrote that in Martha's absence, smoking twenty-five cigarettes a day was simply a human need for narcosis. By burying himself in work and other activities, he protected himself from his sensitivity and excitability. This frenzied work pace led him to cocaine, which he counted on to become famous and financially independent. He used the drug to overcome his anxiety and shyness of public speaking or to boost himself during his long walks, without questioning its potential addictiveness. At the time, he was using it as a stimulant and a prosthesis against his burdensome symptoms.

To what extent do these letters shed light on Freud as a young man? "Many of these characteristics no doubt typically appear at the end of adolescence: lack of self-control, experiences of extreme exaltation and deep despair, sometimes striking contradictions, anxious searching, accelerated pace" (Ibid. p. 792). Exaltation followed by despair necessarily reminds us of the alternation between idealisation and manic excitement, followed by disappointment and depression.

Six months after the last letter from this first period of their relationship, the letters sent to Martha's younger sister Minna show a more serene, solid and controlled Freud, cheerfully writing that his relationship with Martha has never been better, or that the existential security has now been reached. We read these as attesting to Freud slowly gaining a more profound sense of inner security. Among the qualities that appear, we note the extreme openness of his senses, which encouraged originality of thought and creativity. Together with his kind of personal vulnerability, these characteristics were key to Freud's gradual turning towards psychology and psychopathology, which encouraged his increasingly more radical self-exploration, Grubrich-Simitis and Lortholary argue, referring to Freud's self-analysis, already present in his relationship with Eduard.

3.2   Opening a space for desire

Freud only had six occasions to visit his fiancée, usually for no more than a few days. When they were apart, he would write to her almost daily. Speaking of a walk in Prater, a popular park in Vienna, he returned to their first romantic exchange during a family outing organised by Jacob Freud, "our old man" (Freud, 1873–1939, p. 22). "The day aroused memories pleasant in themselves, but melancholy in their recurrence." He then recalled that it was there in the Prater that they had grown fonder of each other day by day. They had eaten and drunk beer together, they "had even pressed each other's hands" and he could no longer wait for the moment of leaving, a moment of feverish closeness. Because of his shyness, he rarely kissed her,

> because as yet I could not quite grasp what has now become the first and most natural condition of my life: that I had suddenly won for myself a unique, incomparable girl. Oh, the Prater is a paradise indeed; only the Wandsbek grove is more beautiful because there we were alone like Adam and Eve, except for a number of animals (which were harmless enough),

he remembered.

The link between love and nature is nothing new in Freud's prose. In this passage it includes an admission: of never before having understood the importance of a love relationship. "Suddenly" winning an idealised girl reminds us of his infatuation with Gisela, but this time love comes with a more realistic prospect, in the sense that sexual repression leaves space for the wish to find emotional fulfilment as a man.

After some weeks of a discreet, secret and intense love affair, Freud suggested in a letter a tender and furtive secret handshake, probably the one he alludes to in his memory of Prater. He was impatient and wanted to get married as soon as possible. Looking back, he never mentioned this sense of urgency, despite the great many personal anecdotes present in his writings. Here again, all references to his romantic feelings were censored. He had no issue presenting himself as a villain, a parricidal son, as ambitious, vindictive and even petty, but never as romantic, as a lover, unless we count the few discreet allusions to his fiancée and later wife. As for the Gisela episode, it was disguised as a clinical case.

Until this time, literature and science were overinvested at the cost of any romantic relationship. The psycho-sexual conflict central to Freud's adolescence nevertheless gave way in his desire to seduce Martha, who had other suitors. As in all matters of the heart, discretion was key: they secretly got engaged on 27th June 1882 and decided to comply with the conventions of the time, forcing them into a long period of premarital chastity. Roudinesco adds that while other young men of Freud's generation frequented brothels or maintained liaisons with married women, "Freud chose abstinence, drugs, Romantic exaltation and sublimation." In his letters to Martha, he

> showed himself to be by turns tyrannical, impetuous, jealous, melancholic, prolific, and capable of working out projects for daily life in minute detail, to the point of describing in advance how he saw the organisation of his future household. Martha was to be his sweet princess, he declared, the one to whom countless gifts and elegant clothes would be offered. But she would also be obliged to restrict her activities to house management and the education of the children, and to turn her back on any project of emancipation. On every page Freud contradicted the theses of John Stuart Mill, despite the fact that he himself had translated a work by Mill devoted to the freedom of women.
>
> (Roudinesco, 2016, p. 36)

This tension, already represented in his letters to Silberstein, between a fairly modern position on women's emancipation and one that was closer to the bourgeois morality of his time, relied on two ideas of women: the free woman associated with the image of the whore and the housewife resembling the mother. Between anxieties and frustrations, these four premarital years were Freud's "Werther period", as Eissler puts it (1978). The reference to Goethe's novel is not accidental: both the author and the book were part of the pantheon of idols of Freud's boyhood; the work is also a classic account of adolescent romantic torment. The contrast between the passionate tone of his letters to Martha and the boyish shyness he described is therefore all the more striking. Of course, we can agree with Eissler's idea of Freud's "silent maturation" over the ten years separating Gisela from Martha, but only on the condition of also noticing the persistent emotional immaturity of an inhibited young man, still prey to his phobic tendencies towards women.

At twenty-seven, Freud left the family home for the first time to live alone, while continuing to spend most of his weekends in the company of his family and his books. To Martha, he wrote poetically about his new apartment: "That said, there is room in the smallest cottage for a solitary being – and one who desires."

3.3 Neurotic misery

On meeting his future wife, Freud was suffering from inhibitions, anxiety, neurasthenia and various psychosomatic problems: colitis, different aches and pains, heart and digestive issues, inflammatory neuralgias, migraines and fainting. His body, which he called "poor Conrad", never seemed to leave him at peace. "To be healthy is so wonderful if one isn't condemned to be alone", he wrote to Martha (Freud, 1873–1939, p. 142) – and yet he was often both alone and ill. The fact that solitude was experienced as a kind of punishment suggests that although his interest in girls had been occluded by his commitment to academics, this absence did not weigh on him any less heavily. Incestuous fantasies functioned as an obstruction and carried a cruel punishment – being alone, or the sad resignation of being deprived of or excluded from the experience of his peers. To Fluss he wrote that he was happy to imagine what others must be living.

His letters to Martha were an opportunity to speak about himself more personally and reflect on his past. In retrospect, the depressive and self-deprecating feelings seem to greatly intensify Freud's sense of unhappiness before meeting his fiancée, contrary to the somewhat megalomaniac positions we glimpse in his letters to Eduard. Just to give an example: "In my youth I was never young" (Ibid., p. 202), he wrote. Or: "I have always restrained myself" and "Before I met you I didn't know the joy of living" (p. 112), alluding to his deep despair, which at another moment he described as: "[if] I hadn't found you . . . I would just have strayed miserably about and gone into a decline" (p. 57). Based on these, I have previously written that Freud saw Martha as his saviour (Houssier, 2018a). Though he had expected to be saved by a figure of benevolent authority, it was his meeting with her that was now associated with this fantasy. There is no need repeat that despite his academic and professional achievements, Freud's solitary and abstinent youth was painful. However, one element, which reminds us of the "principles", a term shared with Eduard, deserves to be mentioned: "Before I met you I didn't know the joy of living, and now that 'in principle' you are mine, to have you completely is the one condition I make to life, which I otherwise don't set any great store by" (Freud, 1873–1939, p. 112).

Freud now felt his poverty even more keenly than before: as the future head of a family, he confided in Martha that he could not keep money for himself and leave his sisters Dolfi and Rosa starving, and was planning to give them at least half of what he was earning. He wrote that his former professor of religion and now friend Hammerschlag had helped him with a small sum, and not for the first time. Hammerschlag had already saved him in some difficult situations as a student, which initially made him uncomfortable. Now in possession of fifty florins, Freud wanted to share some of it with his family, which Hammerschlag protested during their conversation, but Freud explained the situation to him, specifically his sisters' need to find work. "Each visit at home naturally makes me slightly melancholy. . . . There's not a penny at home," he wrote in 1884 and again in 1885 (Grubrich-Simitis, Lortholary, 2012, p. 790). In the letter of 5th June 1884, he described his father, unable to work, as having fallen into a "happy state of needlessness and unimportance", while in November 1884 he spoke about his often poorly mother as a woman who "only sees doom and gloom and unfortunately also voices it", while their children were thin and neglected. Because of his constant debts, the humiliations of this vital dependency provoked rage and cynicism, which we also feel in these letters.

3.4   Feeling unappreciated

Having understood that he was in fact not a genius, Freud could no longer see how he may have wanted to become one; he even felt a lack of talent. He considered his capacity for work rather to do with his character and an absence of serious intellectual flaws, as well as his stubbornness. This did not prevent him from feeling superior to Nothnagel and perhaps on par with Charcot. The fact that his castration complex pertained precisely to this question, i.e., being deprived of the genius he would have loved to possess, is hardly surprising. However, the developmental crisis of this period suggests that the clash between his teenage fantasies, soaked in the primordial ink of the "Golden Sigi", and the reality of his struggle to make a name for himself was indeed a shock. The depressive tone of this confrontation is part of the process of the end of adolescence, where the need not to mistake one's desires for reality encourages more realistic and hence more achievable perspectives and projects. He wrote:

> It has taken me so long to win my friends, I have had to struggle so long for my precious girl, and every time I meet someone I realize that an impulse, which defies analysis, leads that person to underestimate me.
>
> (Freud, 1873–1939, p. 199)

This new avatar of his castration complex – being seen as small, as less than others – appeared as a legacy of his disappointments with his teachers. Instead of seeing his potential, the reactions he perceived as rivalrous or aggressive reminded him of his position as a child ignored by his father, recalling his childhood story of wetting the parents' bed (Houssier, 2018a). When Martha reproached him for being gruff with strangers, he responded:

> It is simply the result of suspicion due to my having learned that common or bad people treat me badly, but this is bound to disappear to the extent to which I grow stronger and more independent, and don't have to fear them any more.
>
> (Ibid., Freud, 1873–1939, p. 202)

Was this rivalry and his experience of failure and humiliation linked to what his teachers felt was the young man's burning ambition? From now on, however, his struggle for independence was offset by the joyfulness of what life had unexpectedly gifted to him:

> But when I think what I would be like now if I hadn't found you – lacking ambition, lacking the joy in the lighter pleasures of the world, lacking any fascination with the magic of gold, and endowed at the same time with very moderate intellectual and no material means whatever – I would just have strayed miserably about and gone into a decline.
>
> (Ibid., p. 57)

Martha gave him an aim, a direction, as well as happiness, which made his situation less lamentable; she gave him hope and certainty of success. It was thanks to her that he became a courageous and self-confident man, contrary to his previous experience of being cut off from his ambitions and unable to enjoy a relationship with a woman.

"How bold one gets when one is sure of being loved!" he wrote (Ibid., p. 11), telling Martha that she had also been making him lazy. He had been unable to even look at a book – his bibliophilia gave in to the love-object and its place in Freud's psychic life. He added that he did not enjoy fiction but knew a beautiful fairy tale he had himself experienced. Lofty science could not compete – it had never looked kindly upon him, never said a comforting word, but he now meant more to Martha than he did to science. She repaid him every service a hundredfold and had only him as a servant.

However, his phobia of women also accentuated a lack of trust in his own abilities, quite contrary to the Oedipal wish of becoming a great man. The path to greatness was thus all the steeper because of his complicated relationship to women and the need to fight amidst the harsh reality of conflicting ambitions, far from the daydreams of grandeur shared with Eduard. We can see the entire period between the late 1870s and early 1880s as a confrontation between Freud's ideals and the need to adjust to reality, a conflict which resulted in intense suffering, especially in the sexual field. Between 1884 and 1887, romantic exaltation played a key role in Freud's cocaine consumption, due to his efforts to fend off his neurasthenia and the devastating effects of his sexual abstinence. As for the latter, let us note, for example, that when Fritz Wahle, a friend from Freud's teenage years and now an attractive artist, gave Martha a kiss, Freud reacted by becoming greatly domineering and trying to ban his fiancée from having any contact with his rival. Likewise, he became cross when she visited one of her girlfriends who had been intimate with her fiancée before marriage. Connecting the two events, he wrote about the friend, Elise, that this was the kind of thing that nearly convinced him to drop her, when Fritz Wahle tried to assert his claims on her. Love and abandonment were again closely related. This combined with another source of anxiety. During his study of hereditary mental diseases, he suggested to Martha that there was a neuropathological taint on his mother's side of the family: his uncle was an epileptic, and he, his sister Rosa and his half-brother Emanuel have a "nicely developed tendency toward neurasthenia" (p. 210). As a neurologist, he was worried by such things "as a sailor is by the sea" (Ibid.), without realising that he had implied his mother was the source of this supposedly genetic neurasthenia. Nevertheless, we see that the axis of his desires had changed: their romantic encounter and his desire for independence were now intimately linked.

3.5   Fleischl, between rivalry and admiration

The need for exclusivity with Martha existed alongside his other friendships, which at times continued to trouble him. Contrary to what was at stake with Eduard, these were essentially not horizontal but imbued with the respect and idealisation characteristic of a more vertical relationship. Speaking of his colleague and friend Ernst Fleischl von Marxow, whom, Freud wrote, he had always seen as his ideal, his tone was more sad than aggressive. While he had been able to "enjoy his value and abilities" in their friendship, since meeting Martha, he no longer envied him, because in the meantime Fleischl had fallen out with his fiancée. He imagined however "what a setting [Fleischl] could provide for this jewel", i.e., Martha, fantasising about Fleischl taking her to the Alps, to Venice or Rome. What he envied his colleague had to do specifically with Fleischl's financial independence, compared to his own poverty. "I was compelled painfully to visualize how easy it could be for him – who spends two months of each year in Munich and frequents the most exclusive society – to meet Martha at her uncle's" (Ibid., p. 12), he concluded, conveying the degree to which his poverty tormented him and made him feel inferior. Again, in his mind, his jealousy worked to his detriment: Martha may have quite naturally been attracted to a rich and brilliant man such as Fleischl, making Freud worry that he was again losing against another, and would be abandoned or rejected due to his financial precariousness, a fear his love for Martha only accentuated. He also told her that his friend was very enthusiastic about his work and promised Freud that if his discovery succeeded, he would help him financially until he too had had a breakthrough (Ibid., p. 73). Freud did not take this promise seriously but considered it a sign of the "warmth of our relationship". In a letter to Martha from 27th June 1882, he described Fleischl as a distinguished and highly educated man, "with the stamp of genius in his manly features, good-looking, refined, endowed with many talents and capable of forming an original judgment about most things" (Ibid., p. 11) – qualities he himself felt deprived of.

As part of this idealisation, he added in a letter from October 1883: "I admire him and love him with an intellectual passion, if I may put it that way. His death will affect me like the destruction of a sacred temple would have a Greek of antiquity." Fleischl was already suffering from a terminal illness and Freud was preparing for another loss. Moreover, his bisexual openness, or at least an openness to intense friendships with a homosexual dimension, was disguised as an intellectual passion, where intellectualisation served as a defence against homosexual fantasies.

Striving towards his future success with this new sentimental endeavour, being in love and having to remain sexually abstinent made Freud at times unbearable, despotic and irrational (Roudinesco, 2016, p. 36); however, in his letters to his fiancée the descriptions of his difficulties seem coloured by despair rather than anger. The libidinal fixation on the auto-erotic cathexes of his adolescence had shifted, giving the drive a new aim: he now wished to work and save in order to "deserve" his happiness with Martha.

His sexual inhibitions and frustrations also had an important underside – they brought out a fantasy of success, which was now quite distinct from his professional achievements. Despite all the romantic tensions, this fantasy was now the source of a new ambition, namely, to win Martha for good.

3.6   Dream or reality? Dream and reality

This new romantic project nevertheless involved a number of concerns. He wanted Martha to "keep young and fresh as long as possible" (Freud, 1873–1939, p. 12). To help him bear their separation, he imagined her as a "round, rosy-cheeked girl" (p. 15). In the poem celebrating Gisela's marriage, he had previously endorsed feminine beauty and its forms. In a later letter, Freud asked if Martha would happily wait for him for fifteen years; he imagined her as a thirty-year-old and promised to see her as young as when he first met her, in fact even younger, because at the time she gave a "matronly" impression. "But will you really remain as young as that?" (p. 94), he wondered, as if echoing his own reluctance to accept ageing. Despite this anxiety, the beginnings of their relationship were largely coloured by Freud's idealisation, to the extent that his sense of reality sometimes wavered, reminding us of his later text on *The Uncanny* and its series of moments of derealisation (Freud, 1919), between dream, fantasy and reality. In their study of Freud's personality, Grubrich-Simitis and Lortholary (2012, p. 792) notice "the extreme permeability of the boundaries of his ego", which continuously put at risk his inner equilibrium.

Certain passages of Sigmund and Martha's courtship letters describe the uncanny effects of their encounter and the separation that followed. The letter of 14th July 1882 (Freud, 1873–1939, p. 7) initially highlights how difficult this separation was. Had he not had her picture in front of him, he would have thought it was "all a beguiling dream" and would be afraid to wake up. Something here reminds us of the refusal to believe in something too beautiful to be true, such as what he felt before the Acropolis (Freud, 1936). "Yet friends tell me it's true", he wrote, emphasising the intensity of what he had long felt deprived of and which escaped him just as he was about to reach his goal. Fortunately, he could rely on his memory of certain details, which were "more mysteriously enchanting than any dream phantasy" (Freud, 1873–1939, p. 8).

His story of their love affair was as follows: from their first meeting and despite his resistances, Martha conquered his heart, while he had been too afraid to court her. It was her who approached him, strengthened his confidence and gave him new hope, a new force to work when he needed it most. He felt shy and awkward in her presence; he dreamt of sitting at her feet, her in an armchair, him on a stool, and no intrusions from without nor farewells nor worries would keep them apart. He would not kiss her nor speak to her in front of a stranger. As a knight, he would arrive without weapons, having left poison and dagger at home for a rival. Like a devoted servant, he wanted to protect and defend her from both enemies and friends (Ibid., p. 15). He had funny thoughts when writing to her – but not just thoughts, sometimes actions, too. With his usual candour, he told her that sometimes he would spot a young girl in the street, someone who reminded him of Martha, and would follow the stranger to make sure it wasn't her – a story fitting of one of E.T.A. Hoffman's tales (Freud, 1919).

Moreover, looking at her photograph, he expected one of her arms to leave the frame and take his hand. Rather than showing it alongside the photographs of the severe faces of the men he admired, he kept the delicate face of the girl he loved locked away, worried that in his absence it might escape him (Freud, Freud, 1873–1939, p. 8). When he would fall asleep and then wake up again in the middle of the night, he had to quickly dismiss the idea that he could have gone blind, and would rush to the window to make sure he had not been punished like Oedipus before him (Ibid., p. 230).

The possibility of fulfilling his sexual wishes associated with the loss of the girl he had successfully won over surrounded their relationship like a halo, softening the boundary between fantasy and reality. In finding again his primal object, both possible and impossible for a child or a baby, Freud both saw himself as the recipient of a miracle, idealising his saviour, and, out of guilt, struggled to accept this gift, resulting in inner conflict. Failing to accept reality or being punished thus became part of the series of expressions of his sense of guilt.

3.7   Fleeing the Sirens

In one letter, he referred to "The New Melusina", an extract from Goethe's *Wilhelm Meister's Wanderings*, a fairy tale that reminded him of several aspects of his relationship with Martha. Given the newness of their love union, the return of the figure of the apprentice is no surprise to us. However, his later analysis of one of his dreams provides more clues to Freud's reference (1901a). The dream features a swimming pool, where the bathers appear to be fleeing in all directions. At one point, a person is standing on the edge of the pool and bending towards someone bathing, as if to help her out of the water.

> The situation was put together from a memory of an experience I had had at puberty and from two paintings, one of which I had seen shortly before the dream. One was a picture from Schwind's series illustrating the legend of Mélusine, which showed the water-nymphs surprised in their pool (cf. the scattering bathers in the dream); the other was a picture of the Deluge by an Italian Master; while the little experience remembered from my puberty was of having seen

the instructor at a swimming-school helping a lady out of the water who had stopped in until after the time set aside for men bathers.

(Freud, 1901a, p. 649)

Anzieu argues that the theme of the dream is the boy's curiosity about female nudity and its perils. Nevertheless, the myth of *Mélusine* is richer still. In the story, a girl is struck by a maternal curse, which revolves around a prohibition: she cannot be seen naked one day in the week, or her future husband might discover that she has a fishtail like a Siren. Here, Freud identifies with the husband-to-be, discovering his fiancée's secret. Infantile sexual curiosity adds to the intensity of what he later called pubertal curiosity (Freud, 1905b), the thirst for sexual explanations, or the desire to be helped in discovering genital sexuality, given the fantasies of feminine dangers portrayed by the myth.

Note specifically the flood that swallows all – like the primordial mother or the Siren, a woman hiding a tail, who in the myth represents a danger to the hypnotised sailors. Freud returned to more realistic ideas when he associated the dream with caressing his fiancée's hand under the table, as a shy and modest young man belatedly discovering carnal pleasures. When he told Martha to be patient about their future marriage, he added that, saying so "forgets how things get lost when we cannot have them then and there, when we have to pay for them with our own youth" (Freud, 1873–1939, p. 24).

In a subsequent letter, he again returned to the Melusine myth and the prohibitions against seeing and touching he felt during his adolescence. Freud later emphasised that in the unconscious, seeing and touching were united as thinking and doing (Freud, 1901a). Curiosity thus added to the intensity of the sexual desires which the scantily clad bodies of the bathers allowed him to glimpse, between lust and shame. Let's add also that the woman he sees coming out of the pool is older, possibly closer to his mother's age. The sight of his mother's naked body was interpreted by Freud as the central source of his sexual desires; he later argued that one of the typical fantasies of adolescence was to be sexually initiated by one's mother (Freud, 1908). These dreams, myth, literary references and the fantasy of initiation all suggest that the experiences forming the associative juncture between Freud's dream and the relationship with his fiancée were highly charged. The sight of the fleeing bathers attests to a disorganising experience of guilt when confronted with the eroticised vision of the naked female body. The scene of panic in the face of a maternal figure is triangulated by the male figure helping the woman out of the water, i.e., another source of guilt in this scene *à trois*. The dream illustrates the way in which adolescence brings intense Oedipal anxieties back to the surface, combining them with more primitive anxieties (engulfment, undifferentiation, the non-castrated maternal figure).

"What sorceresses you women are!" Freud also wrote to Martha (Freud, 1873–1939, p. 9), after having been so interested in witches in his correspondence with Silberstein. And by the way, to live happily, one must live hidden: he wanted to prevent raising any suspicions about his amorous state by continuing to socialise with the girls around Martha's brother Eli and Ignaz Schonberg, Minna's fiancée of four years, even though he would rather be alone. "I drug myself with work", he wrote, even before he started experimenting with cocaine. "That is how exclusive I am when I love" (Ibid.), he pointed out, portraying himself as a poor man who had been made blissfully happy by her. However, he also wrote, in the summer of 1882, that he found it "uncanny" only to be able to understand the emotional lives of others on the basis of his own (Grubrich-Simitis, Lortholary, 2012, p. 796).

3.8   Forcing oneself on her to recognise his loved one

Because Freud was convinced that he was more in love with Martha than she was with him, he reproached her for having consented to their engagement without a genuine desire and complained of how it made him suffer. Just like with Eduard, looking for completeness in a unity with another person, where differences were reduced, reminds us of Freud's search for his twin double. In June 1884, he wrote, as if to present a case:

> I forced myself upon you and you accepted me without any great affection. I know it has finally changed and this success, which I wanted more than anything else, and the prolonged absence of which has been my greatest misery, gives me hope for the other successes which I still need.
>
> (Freud, 1873–1939, p. 117)

He added:

> How we were always fighting, and you would never give in to me? We were two people who diverged in every detail of life and who were yet determined to love each other and did love each other. And then, after no hard words had been exchanged between us for a long time, I had to admit to myself that you were indeed my beloved, but so seldom took my side that no one would have realized from your behaviour that you were preparing to share my life.
>
> (Ibid.)

But once the conflicts had dissipated, he was again looking for the enemy, and began hating Martha's mother Emmeline for being the cause of their separation. The feelings were mutual. Contrary to the Gisela episode, this time Freud was determined to separate mother from daughter, the former revealed to be just as diabolical as the one who stirred his jealousy in the conflict with Eduard. Again, the mother-daughter dyad excluding him was the object of harsh criticism: he blamed Martha's mother for resembling a man and having deprived him of Martha by leaving Vienna for Wandsbek. He openly mocked her obscurantist religious rituals and repeatedly called on Martha to get away from her, with thinly veiled reproaches. The angry threats he made against his wife-to-be came alongside comparisons between her and her sister. He considered that even though Martha showed her mother respect, she hardly had any love for her; on the contrary, Minna adored their mother, but spared her no criticism. Speaking about the "matron's" departure in August 1882, he again threatened Martha that were he to go without seeing her for more than two weeks, his egotism would rise up against "Mama and Eli-Fritz and I will make such a dit that everyone will hear and understand" (p. 23). And when Martha would return, he insisted, it would be back to him, no matter her filial feelings, a kind of forced separation. He called upon the tradition that since time immemorial had been laid down, that a woman shall leave father and mother and follow the man she's chosen, since no filial love could compare to his own. The rivalrous tension between familial and extrafamilial attachment is patent here.

His criticism of Martha's mother was intense and aggressive, and at times full of projection. In his mind, Frau Bernays was demanding to fully partake in life by remaining centre stage; her only goal was to dominate. She was jealous of the feelings of others from which she was excluded. She insisted on living in Wandsbek without any consideration for her two daughters or their respective fiancés, who had both remained in Vienna. These demands of the elderly – which Freud normally associated with men and was surprised to find in a woman – expressed an eternal conflict between the old and the young present in every family, in which no one wanted to be sacrificed and everyone wished to follow their own way and do as they please.

Although he admitted that while Martha's mother acted unjustly, he did not consider her a stranger, he wrote that he did not expect much from her. After all, it was not her he had chosen to marry – a rather Oedipal negation, disregarding his at times genuine fascination with mother-daughter couples.

He believed that his separation from Martha required regular contact. If she had not written for more than two days, he would be desperate to hear from her. In these moments of hunger for the object, he would forbid himself thinking of her too much, or he was afraid of losing his patience, which he indeed needed to tolerate the whole situation – here again he spoke of his crises of hypochondria and despair. Once again separated from his beloved, his violent criticism of Martha's mother reminds us of the mother at the origin of his own primordial losses. We have seen that Freud's own mother was not particularly available to him as a child, not just due to her subsequent pregnancies but also her bereavement after the death of Freud's brother Julius. Moreover, Freud's love for his nanny, who was arrested for theft at the moment of his sister's Anna's birth, was also followed by the loss of his niece Pauline leaving for England.

3.9 Abandonment, between unfaithfulness and disloyalty

Hardin (1987) sees the difficulty of finding a mother substitute in this series of losses as Freud's fundamental question, linked to his persistent fear of abandonment. It also hindered him from forming a genuine attachment to a woman and provoked his excessive use of a defensive feigned independence.

As a teenager, Freud was forced to conceal his desire for passive dependence behind the mask of premature self-confidence. His superego was reinforced by his wish for exclusiveness, combined with his incestuous and transgressive desires. The fantasies of deflowering and rape stem from his sexual frustration but also a wish to retain control over an object constantly escaping him; hence his passionate reactions towards Martha and her mother. With his fiancée, he felt bold and courageous; however, after one of their disagreements, he wrote to her that he was glad she was no longer cross with him, because the idea of losing her love gave him a strange feeling of forlornness (Freud, 1873–1939, p. 197).

He also developed little tolerance of his friends' "infidelity", the lack of loyalty he felt his colleagues showed towards himself and later the psychoanalytic cause – another version of his feeling of abandonment. This desire for exclusivity in his close relationships, illustrated by his friendship with Eduard, also appeared when he perceived Martha's brother as a rival. He accused his brother-in-law Eli Bernays of making dodgy transactions, while Eli had in fact been blackmailed by a woman who claimed to bear his child. Martha courageously took her brother's side, even when Freud accused him of being a scoundrel. Eli's marriage to Anna, Freud's sister whom he disdained, put an end to this hostility. It did not prevent Freud from writing, apropos visiting his fiancée in Wandsbek, that she was being held there by his "enemies" or wishing they could greet each other "unwitnessed by other human eyes", without her cousin Max who had previously been one of Martha's suitors (Ibid., p. 14). Like with Eduard, he believed they did not need a third person between them: in their necessarily exclusive relationship, anyone else could only be a rival or an intruder. "I think you should be a little more jealous of [Schonberg]; it should never come to the point where your relationship with him can be clouded by that to any third person", he also wrote to Martha's sister Minna, presuming Martha's mother to be just as intrusive towards Minna's relationship with her fiancée. On the contrary, regarding himself and Martha he praised "our system of closing ourselves off", which put them in a better position: "We have no intention of sharing the painful pleasure of stirred-up passions, we have a practical aim: to live and work together" (Ibid., p. 39). He wondered how to make Martha less attractive so that no one would fall in love with her. "True, the tyrannical temperament that makes little girls afraid of me could not be subdued. I wanted exclusiveness. . . . My girl came from a family of scholars, and wrote – for the time being only letters – with untiring hand", he also wrote. He chose a notepaper on which she could only write to him, with the letters M and S intimately entwined, resulting in a "despotic paper" (Ibid, p. 18). A distant echo of the seal of the Spanish Academy: two letters forming a distinctive sign, a secret code to express the need to be alone with one's beloved.

3.10 Minna, another double?

Freud would sometimes try to find refuge in Minna, whose judgment he considered more independent than Martha's. This doubling created a new extended family: Minna became Martha's "educated" double, with the two female images coupled together at the centre of Freud's life. In 1883, Minna became engaged to Freud's friend Ignaz Schonberg. Freud saw her as an intelligent and sharp-witted girl, calling her "my dear, my sister" in their correspondence. He was convinced that Minna resembled him, that she was just as passionate; physically, she may have been her sister's twin. He was hopeful the two couples could create a kind of fraternal bond, but in 1885 Schonberg died of tuberculosis. This bisexual fraternity again included the idea of a twin-like relationship, this time between the two sisters loved by Freud. This narcissistic dimension was also present in his relationship with Martha, to whom he wrote, while waiting for her in sad resignation, "the nicest thing about [life] is what one grants oneself in secret, as I am doing now" (Ibid., p. 10).

In her absence, Martha was placed on a pedestal; notwithstanding certain expressions of ambivalence, Freud constantly reassured her of his faithfulness and love. However, after they were married, Freud did become more emotionally distant, just like he was with most women, except for his sister-in-law Minna (Hamilton, 2002). Their intimate friendship has been commented on in great detail, sometimes including speculations of a possible sexual relationship. However, if we only think of Freud's tendency to sublimate sexual conflicts, his wish to be surrounded by a large family to avoid his feelings of abandonment or his tendency to create these emotional doubles to represent the two images of his mother – eroticised and chaste, idealised and despised – an explicitly erotic relationship with Minna seems less likely.

When he wrote to Minna after the death of her fiancé, he expressed his sympathies and support. Only just having left girlhood behind, she had to take on responsibilities normally reserved for adults. He encouraged her to try and regain some of this lost youth during which one was only meant to focus on growth and development. He suggested that she give her emotions a long rest and live for some time with him and Martha, two people now closest to her. He also advised her to burn Schonberg's letters she had received that winter, in order to help her forget and move on (Freud, 1873–1939, p. 205). By pointing out such overly abrupt transitions from childhood to adulthood, Freud again implicitly recognised the importance of adolescence in human life. Regaining one's youth and consecrating it by burning one's letters or the idea of burning the painful memories of one's youth were both among the typical tropes of Freud's personality, during adolescence and beyond.

3.11   Cocaine and sense of duty

Why should we be interested in Freud's cocaine episode? First of all because it shows us an attempt to demonstrate his talents in the field of scientific research. Freud was very preoccupied with avoiding his father's fate by making himself a name. He wrote to Martha: "As you know, an explorer's temperament requires two basic qualities: optimism in attempt, criticism in work" (Ibid., p. 108). Secondly, because the cocaine episode appears in a chain of associations as a reference to Freud's adolescence. Freud wrote to Fritz Wittels, his first unofficial biographer (1924), that his research on cocaine was an "allotrion". Bernfeld (1953) explains this term by referring to Freud's teachers, who used it pejoratively for everything that detracted from doing one's duty in favour of leisure or mischief. Etymologically, *allotrion* means "a stranger to oneself", in the sense of turning away from one's designated path. Bernfeld adds that the four years of Freud's engagement were the least productive research-wise, which echoes Freud's own conviction that his obsession with Gisela Fluss had hindered his creativity.

He also wrote to Martha that only a suffering man was able to accomplish great things and that when he was filled with happiness, he could neither create nor think. The study of cocaine was also part of Freud's interest in plants, a series of which he studied as a young man. It represented his first attempt at doing independent research, even though it was not until the 1890s that his thought reached its maturity and freed itself from mainstream perspectives.

Just as a reminder of the context, Freud found an article in a scientific journal, the *Detroit Medical Gazette*, on the use of coca in the treatment of morphine addicts. This gave him hope of being able to help his friend Fleischl, whose right hand had to be amputated following a work injury. After a whole series of operations, Fleischl became addicted to morphine. In May 1884, Freud persuaded him to experiment with large doses of cocaine; Fleischl's reaction was such that Freud had to repeatedly rush to his side throughout the night to try and calm him down. Fleischl remained addicted to cocaine until his death on 22nd October 1891 (Hamilton, 2002).

Freud self-medicated with cocaine to fight his neurasthenia, an anxio-depressive illness on which he later commented in his letters to Fliess (Freud, 1887–1904) to say that it mostly affected young men engaging in masturbation. Before he understood the toxicity of cocaine, Freud thought it had important euphoric effects which could treat his depressive moods. He also told Martha that he considered her opinion when he decided to refuse being ill. He then spoke about his neurasthenia as a result of overwork, stress and emotional upheaval of the recent years, which would disappear as if by magic every time he was with his beloved. In her absence, cocaine provided manic anti-depressive excitement supposedly boosting his creativity.

His sense of duty, sustained by the tyranny of the superego through a series of self-reproaches, was in constant conflict with his desire not to engage in anything serious. After studying in the laboratory, he nevertheless became focused exclusively on cocaine, hoping for an original discovery. Lack of willpower and thoroughness were among his usual self-reproaches, going back to his adolescence, when he would also berate himself regularly for daydreaming, wasting time or losing himself in various literary or scientific explorations at the expense of concentrating on fulfilling his ambitions.

The dream of the botanical monograph refers to cocaine and illustrates this conflict: "once, I recalled, I really *had* written something in the nature of a *monograph on a plant*, namely a dissertation on the *coca-plant*, which had drawn Karl Koller's attention to the anaesthetic properties of cocaine" (Freud, 1900, p. 170, original emphasis). Freud adds that like the dream of Irma's injection, this dream too has the character of self-justification, a plea on his behalf.

> What it meant was: "After all, I'm the man who wrote the valuable and memorable paper (on cocaine)", just as in the earlier dream I had said on my behalf: "I'm a conscientious and hard-working student." In both cases what I was insisting was: "I may allow myself to do this."
>
> (Ibid., p. 173)

The work of adolescence is palpable in this series of self-authorisations, which imply the need to tolerate one's guilt for choosing a path different from one's predecessors, teachers or substitute fathers, slowly disinvesting them of their power. This symbolic movement of murdering the guardian figure brings more self-confidence and creates trust in being able to become the master of one's destiny, rather than a student subject to the gaze of a teacher, as aptly illustrated by the scenario with Brücke. Freud's meeting with Martha accentuated this shift, despite the persistence of certain traces of conflict. Intertwined with his daydreams of grandeur, the final part of Freud's adolescent journey was now directed towards this post-Oedipal perspective: "Now it's my turn to become a master." Having access to a love relationship which included difference and ambivalence played a key role in the integration of this ever-malleable position.

3.12   New temptations: first signs of ambivalence

Freud's ambivalence towards Martha later appeared in his analysis of certain dreams, for instance when he compared her to his patient Irma:

> I was forced to admit to myself that I was not treating either Irma or my wife very kindly in this dream; but it should be observed by way of excuse that I was measuring them both by the standard of the good and amenable patient.
>
> (Freud, 1900, p. 110, n1)

Freud did not just compare his wife to a patient; he wrote about his admiration for Martha's intellect in October 1883: "You're writing so precisely and intelligently that I am a little afraid of you. I told myself that it shows, once again, how a woman quickly surpasses a man" (Grubrich-Simitis, Lortholary, 2012, p. 788).

This rivalrous ambivalence was much more clearly sexualised when he wrote to his fiancée from Paris. During an evening at the Charcots, Freud at first remained with the men and spoke little to Charcot's twenty-year-old daughter. To Martha he later wrote that had he not been in love already, he would have been strongly tempted to court Mlle Charcot, "for nothing is more dangerous than a young girl bearing the features of a man whom one admires" (Freud, 1873–1939, p. 197). He would then of course become a laughingstock, be thrown out and it would all be a "beautiful adventure" (ibid.), he justified himself. It was better as it was, after all. The anecdote, this time involving a daughter and her admired father, reminds us of the twelve-year-old girl followed by Freud on his train journey, whom he thought resembled a young page. However, the situation is similar yet different: an attraction for the daughter of a teacher is one of the ways of becoming a teacher himself, by "taking" something from the father, namely his daughter. Freud also confided in Martha that he had dreamt she was the daughter of Joseph Breuer, another figure of identification.

More prosaically, from the beginnings of his liaison with Martha, Freud, who said he had never really been young, discovered the games of seduction. As the saying goes, appetite comes with eating. It is not impossible that the fear of being replaced in Martha's affections by another man forced him to reveal his own desires, even though he had already begun to explore his own psychic life. The discovery of genital sexuality was a decisive moment, in the sense that Freud's libido now turned towards a sexualised object rather than yet another sublimated substitute. In July 1883, echoing his later text on the screen memory, he connected sexuality and hunger in his comments on Flaubert's *The Temptation of Saint Anthony*, published nine years prior. Freud compared himself to the famous starving penitent, alluding to the sexual misery imposed by their separation. Seizing a (sexual) opportunity was in fact a recurrent idea for Freud, an infantile resonance becoming meaningful during adolescence, as shown by his analysis of the dream of the three Fates.

3.13   The breast, hunger and love

In Freud's analysis of the dream of the three Fates, the question is not just of a hero who goes mad, calling out the names of the three women "who had brought the greatest happiness and sorrow into his life" (Freud, 1900, p 204). He adds that one of the names was *Pélagie* and added:

> In connection with the three women I thought of the three Fates who spin the destiny of man, and I knew that one of the three women – the inn-hostess in the dream – was the mother who gives life, and furthermore (as in my own case) gives the living creature its first nourishment. Love and hunger, I reflected, meet at a woman's breast.

He continued:

> A young man who was a great admirer of feminine beauty was talking once – so the story went – of the good-looking wet-nurse who had suckled him when he was a baby: "I'm sorry," he remarked, "that I didn't make a better use of my opportunity."

(Ibid.)

Adolescence is here one of the sources of remembering the infantile or indeed the primordial. If it is impossible to infer a baby's experience with his wet-nurse in another way than through the lens of adolescence – finding an object always means finding it again, Freud wrote about puberty (1905a) – Freud is logically speaking about his own youth and his relationship to women when voicing the regret of not having made better use of it as an inhibited and solitary teenager driven by monastic fantasies.

On reading Freud's interpretation of the dream, it is somewhat surprising to find that the terms used by the two main French translations do not actually result in the same meaning. Besides a reference to death, the dream-thought that follows is absent from the most recent translation. In the first version, Freud returns to the image of one Fate by associating it directly with his mother:

> When I was six years old and was given my first lessons by my mother, I was expected to believe that we were all made of earth and must therefore return to earth. . . . For one of the thoughts which my hunger introduced into the dream was this: "One should never neglect an opportunity, but always take what one can even when it involves doing a small wrong. One should never *neglect an opportunity*, since life is short and death inevitable."
>
> (Freud, 1900, pp. 205, 213, my emphasis)

Because this thought also has a sexual meaning, in the sense that desire does not want to be hindered by guilt, this carpe diem is subject to censorship and must be hidden behind a dream. We should add that there is a distancing in the dream account and its associations through a kind of impersonalisation (the dreamer, rather than his own memories). The sensual desire linked to the relationship to his mother awakens the wish to escape mortality by enjoying life, especially sexual life. Missing on one's sexual life thus provokes, by extension, the desire not to miss any opportunity with respect to one's future death, but the sexual dimension insists – taking whatever you can get, even if it might make you feel guilty – reminds us of both incestuous desires and of Freud's moralising admonitions of Silberstein's libertinage, begrudging his friend's ability to take advantage of his opportunities with young women.

Freud nevertheless finds a modest way out. The interpretation of the dream ultimately has a different emphasis, an idea that it would be associated, like someone who has plagiarised, with "the thief who had for some time carried on his business of stealing overcoats in the lecture-rooms" (p. 205). This association leads to Brücke, an important paternal figure in Freud's history. Plagiarising ideas is linked to the fantasy of imitating father in his desire for mother; stealing means appropriating something that belongs to the other, taking the object of one's desire and enjoying it despite this transgression. Given that Brücke was also the person to look reproachfully at Freud when he would arrive late to his laboratory, his penetrating gaze making a lasting impression, it is easy to associate him with a paternal figure able to discipline the guilty party.

However, we can also add the figure of Fliess, who later became the object, in terms hardly more measured, of Freud's previous passion for Silberstein. The plagiarism Freud felt accused of was one of the reasons for their ultimate falling out; Fliess argued that Freud had "stolen" his idea of the generalised psychic bisexuality, which Freud repeatedly refuted. Freud's understanding of adolescence suggests that the question of bisexuality was subjectively indeed his own.

Exploring the rest of this text confirms our interpretation. Freud adds that: "All kinds of thoughts having a *contrary* sense then found voice: memories of a time when the dreamer was content with *spiritual* food, restraining thoughts of every kind and even threats of the most revolting sexual punishments" (p. 208). Spiritual food refers to the maternal world of the Fate preparing the dumplings and giving her first lessons, i.e., the source of desire. However, this is not all; it was during his adolescence that nourishment became spiritual, fuelling the world of daydreams, when Freud became passionately involved in his reading, raising a concern for his father. The rest of the sentence is self-explanatory: sexual desires remobilised by puberty are confronted with terrible threats, which range from inhibitory impediments of anal nature to disgusting sexual punishments. The "contrary" thoughts mark the intensity of young Freud's struggle against his sexual fantasies; the paralysing inhibition worked against the fulfilment of these grandiose, incestuous and heroic fantasies. The long-distance relationship with Martha, together with a fantasy of possession – she belonged to him – took on the entire infantile-juvenile complex, against the backdrop of Freud's regrets of not having sexually taken advantage of his youth.

3.14   Having choices, being free

The most disgusting and shameful incestuous sexual desires were displaced onto an intellectual investment of the world of literature and culture; at the same time, on the emotional front, the wish to remain his mother's favourite child was transformed into a fierce struggle to become a great man, a hero. This trajectory involved a sacrificial aspect in the sexual domain, including Freud's regrets of not having made better use of his youth, as illustrated by another commentary on another autobiographical dream, in a section devoted to punishment dreams.

> In an indistinct part of the background of one of my laboratory dreams I was of an age which placed me precisely in the gloomiest and most unsuccessful year of my medical career. I was still without a post and had no idea how I could earn my living; but at the same time I suddenly discovered that I had a choice open to me between several women whom I might marry! So I was once more young, and, more than everything, *she* was once more young – the woman who had shared all these difficult years with me.
>
> (Freud, 1900, p. 476)

The idea that comes to mind points towards a deep wish to regain his sexual freedom, to have a choice and be able to enjoy several women before marriage, including the once more young Martha.

His commentary on the dream of the botanical monograph also asserts this burning desire for freedom, both internal and external, which echoed his wish to escape later described to Rolland:

> Let us, for instance, take the dream of the botanical monograph. The thoughts corresponding to it consisted of a passionately agitated plea on behalf of my liberty to act as I chose to act and to govern my life as seemed right to me and me alone.
>
> (Freud, 1900, p. 467)

What we can also extract from this passage indicates the intensity of his associations with the dream: "This reminds one of the peace that has descended upon a battlefield strewn with corpses; no trace is left of the struggle which raged over it" (Ibid.). However, this conflict was waged during adolescence and later massively repressed, leaving a battlefield strangely calm in the aftermath of a long internal struggle.

Freud adds another motive, also tainted by regrets or bitterness regarding his adolescent sexuality:

> The unconscious instigator of the dream was thus revealed as one of the constantly gnawing wishes of a man who is growing older. The conflict raging in other levels of the mind between vanity and self-criticism had, it is true, determined the content of the dream; but it was only the more deeply-rooted wish for youth that had made it possible for that conflict to appear as a dream.
>
> (Ibid.)

The wish to regain one's youth and sexual freedom is thus present in the entire series of these dreams or memories, once they have been connected to each other, ideas that prompt a nostalgic addition in 1911: "Even when we are awake we sometimes say to ourselves: 'Things are going very well to-day and times were hard in the old days; all the same, it was lovely then – I was still young'" (Ibid.).

In his dream, Freud finds not just his youth but also the sexual freedom previously denied to him, suggesting that his ambitions contributed to the repression of his sexual wishes. While he is already involved with Martha, the dream allows him to rediscover his youth and a freedom of choice. At a time when he discovered love with Martha, hitherto repressed sensual desires resurfaced as a wish to seduce not one but several women, without having obligations to either of them.

His dreams thus also attest to a related conflict: belonging to Martha and her to him meant having to give up on other women and miss out on the temptations alluded to as missed "opportunities", for example with Charcot's daughter. This idea, linked to the experience he missed out on as a boy and now saw open to him echoed in his encouragement of Martha's patience. Distance accentuated this frustration; far from her, Freud felt that he was constantly forced to keep his feelings under control.

3.15 "Am I still not your confidant?"

Let's return to their letters. The conflicts between the lovers did not disrupt Freud's "sweetest good fortune" (Freud, 1873–1939, p. 24). He asked Martha that she be neither taciturn nor reticent with her discontents, "which we can straighten out and bear together as honest friends and good pals", combining love and friendship without distinction. He did not want to avoid conflicts, even at the price of hurting her feelings, but she should understand this was only to make her his own as intimately as possible, "and if this be egotistical, love after all cannot be anything but egotistical" – an idea to be theorised later.

Friendships remained an important part of his life, even though they were less close than before. He told Martha that all his friends were poor and had promised to help one another, like him and Fleischl, whenever they could. And even when it was impossible to help, he would rarely leave one of them without feeling that the friend had done him some good. The interest they took in him, the hope they placed in him lifted him out of his despondency, offsetting some of the injustice he felt victim to. All of that was of course not as blissful as knowing that one was loved by an exceptional woman, he admitted, but he did not want to give up the moral support of these men, which helped him live, he argued – even though it is unlikely that Martha would have asked for any such renouncement. His friends now functioned the way parental figures used to, helping Freud accept his material situation more easily.

However, his doubts were never too far away. If success corresponded to one's merit, he wondered, would love too not tend to lose some of its purity? How did he know that Martha loved him for himself rather than his professional achievements? And had he been a victim of misfortune, would she no longer love him as his unworthiness would be proven? The Golden Sigi could only feel loved if he proved his value; hence the feeling of injustice linked to misfortune or luck. Love and work were interlinked, despite his belief that true love did not depend on career success. In the end, he demanded Martha to appreciate him without reserve.

In moments of doubt or depression, Freud wrote that he was worried Martha's imagination would lead her to idealise him, yet he wanted to be loved irrationally and regardless of the qualities she attributed to him (p. 89). The idea that she saw him as good-natured provoked a deep-seated rage in him, and a wish to quarrel. This need for conflict appears as a substitute, the desire for an embrace transformed into its opposite. Martha was apparently able to weather these storms without letting herself be pushed around – so that two days later, Freud again felt happy to be alive and working, and less subject to these passionate torments. His imagination at times made him tempestuous and over-critical, for example when he berated Martha for her friendship with Elise, who it turned out had been sexually intimate with her fiancé. Freud was livid: the two of them had promised not to give in to temptation before marriage. He reproached Martha for being too indulgent and never taking offence with her friends. He did not consider himself prudish – which we might find debatable – but this was indeed too much. How come she said nothing to Elise; was she just as careless as her friend? This last admonition perhaps reveals the nature of the wound: he was afraid that Martha might follow Elise's example and leave him for another man. Likewise, he used to fear being abandoned by Silberstein, who would flirt with different girls in Freud's absence. Now he was scared that Elisa's character flaws and lack of restraint might contaminate Martha; he imagined the latter was so bored at home that she might find this friendship a welcome escape, thus becoming estranged from him. "Am I still not your confidant?" he exclaimed (p. 160).

Although calm often came after the storm, it was only apparent, even in the aftermath of their tumultuous long-distance relationship. Returning to this period of his life in 1925, we see a hint of reproach, when Freud designates his fiancée as the reason why he had not become famous at that youthful age. While studying the analgesic properties of cocaine, he asked his friend, the ophthalmologist Leopold Königstein, if the substance could have been used in the treatment of eye disease. He then delayed this research to visit Martha in the midst of their four-year courtship. On returning, he discovered his colleague Carl Koller had already been experimenting with cocaine and had demonstrated its use upon animals' eyes. "[B]ut I bore my *fiancée* no grudge for the interruption" (Freud, 1925, p. 15). Freud argues here in full denial, without recognising the two opposite movements, accusation and exoneration, in his story. The expression that returns – interruption, in the original *Versäumnis*, omission or failure – again reminds us of the missed opportunity, in a series of regrets that concern Freud's marriage, which should have been more financially advantageous, the delayed flourishing of his career, as well as the expression of his sensual desires.

3.16   The Great Cervantes, again and always

The long wait for their marriage caused Freud a kind of "gay moodiness", which he thought prevented him from making good use of his time. He was reading a lot, for example *Don Quixote* with Gustave Doré's illustrations – he wrote that he spent more time with this book, as a substitute for a person, than with brain anatomy. A reminder of his rigid moralism apropos his sisters' education, he wrote to his fiancée that because of the many coarse and nauseating passages, it was certainly not a book for young ladies. He regretted sending it to her and having forgotten about these pages – but rereading those he had recommended he "nearly split my sides, I haven't laughed so much for ages. It is beautifully done" (Freud, 1873–1939, p. 44). He concluded by evoking their love and a competition as to who could be the more loving.

These lines again show us that for Freud, reading was the most delicious pastime, a favourite meal of unparalleled flavours. When he later commented on *Don Quixote*, he said he could not think of any book more pleasant or freer of exaggeration. He took from it the idea that those who lived in reality were in a superior position, poignantly illustrated by the way Sancho falls from the unreal world into reality (p. 45). Did Freud identify with Sancho, who also initially followed his masters and then saw his ideals collapse? Another quixotic fantasy runs through this letter: comparing himself to "our hero", he imagined six students from the course he was teaching kissing Martha's hand, akin to *Don Quixote*, who ordered that the defeated knights kiss the hand of his Dulcinea. This time, Freud could let his chivalrous spirit roam, sharing with Martha his passion for Cervantes, previously so important in his friendship with Eduard.

We see another example of his interest in Spanish culture in a kind of psychological commentary he sent to Martha after seeing a performance of *Carmen*. "The mob gives vent to its appetites, and we deprive ourselves", he wrote, conveying his inner thoughts. To preserve their integrity, health and capacity for enjoyment, the two of them had decided to save themselves "for something, not knowing for what. And this habit of constant suppression of natural instincts gives us the quality of refinement", he commented, adding they should not demand too much of themselves. If they do not get drunk, it is because "the discomfort and disgrace of the after-effects" (Freud, 1873–1939, p. 50) brought more pain than the pleasure of drunkenness. Why not fall in love every month? Because at every separation "a part of our heart would be torn away". Why not make a friend of everyone? Their loss or any misfortune befalling them would affect us deeply, he explained. "Thus we strive more toward avoiding pain than seeking pleasure", he wrote, unaware that he would later theorise the dynamic conflict between the principles of pleasure and reality. For now, the two of them, chained together for life and death, continued to deprive themselves and pining for years to remain faithful (Ibid.).

In these letters, the references to Cervantes or to *Carmen* were not the only ones and German literature was also present:

> I have been reading off and on a few things by the 'mad' Hoffmann, mad, fantastic stuff, here and there a brilliant thought. Once, for instance, a fairy presents a bride with a necklace which has the power of preventing her from ever being annoyed about a greasy spot on her dress or a spoiled soup. Isn't that amusing?
>
> (Ibid., p. 158)

Another aspect emerged when speaking about *Faust* and about the right to be a man and partake in the pleasures of life: chatting to one's love while holding her in one's arms, but also the pleasure of a book that seems to clearly express how we think and feel. Reading as a mirror of one's deepest feelings was indeed one of Freud's most cherished pleasures and using literature to develop his ideas had already become a habit. His love of books never left him and now again took centre stage; he confided in Martha that his bill with his bookseller was "pretty big" (p. 49) and he was all the more glad to establish a personal relationship with him.

3.17   Friendship and love, hand in hand

The courtship letters also gave Freud space to discuss his ideas of romantic love and family in an apparent effort to prepare the ground before committing to marital life.

About to visit to Samuel Hammerschlag, he wrote to Martha that he was excited about the opportunity to speak about her. He added that it seemed completely unrealistic to have women compete with men or be equal to them in the professional sphere, because domestic work, including child-rearing, was a women's affair. As we have already seen, for instance with regards to intelligence and love, rivalry was not absent from Freud's ideas of a couple's life. It was unthinkable for him to push women to have to earn their living as men did, he wrote, or otherwise he would have to think of his sweet girl as a competitor and would make every effort to get her out of this role. If a woman became a competitor, it would lead to the disappearance of the "most lovely thing the world has to offer us: our ideal of womanhood", of beauty, charm and goodness (Freud, 1873–1939, p. 76). After this idealised image, he softened his tone slightly: legislation and custom might give women many more rights of which they had hitherto been deprived, but the position of woman will remain "to be an adored sweetheart in youth, and a beloved wife in maturity" (Ibid.)

Love was conditioned by the fear of abandonment; in the chronicles of their courtship, she had to do all she could not to abandon him, a promise he believed would guarantee her presence. Freud's favourite poem was *Paradise Lost* by Milton. In July 1883, he wrote to Martha:

> I don't know how I came to the idea that each person should choose, among the great and the powerful, a god or a patron to whom they can turn in their saddest and gravest moments. I have chosen John Milton and his sublime enchantment, which is the only thing that can bring me out of the mute and disappointing world of worries, so that Earth becomes a small point in the universe and the vast heavens open.
>
> (Eissler, 2006, p. 96)

Grubrich-Simitis and Lortholary point out that unless there was a health concern, in Freud and Martha's love language, speaking about the face, hands or general appearance were the only ways to evoke the body. On taking a closer look we see that although he did remain fairly prudish, Freud's language did occasionally feature images of the body. Reading between the lines, we glimpse embraces, passionate kisses and real excitement, often after one of Freud's visits to Wandsbek. Sexuality and the erotic tension of their separation were not a source of conflict; distance kept desire for long periods of time in the realm of dreaming and imagination. When Freud shared with Martha that he had climbed the stairs of the Notre-Dame, he talked about the kisses he could have given her at each step, so that she would arrive at the top "out of breath and unbridled".

In my view, the courtship letters that have been translated literally bring an efflorescence of a language of the body, the signs of which were already present in his correspondence with Eduard. "Short steps and a long way, but we will get there all right, and then we will be able to wander on, arm in arm. How lovely that will be!" (Freud, 1873–1939, p. 24). From the memories of his walks with his father to his love affair with Martha, by way of looking for figures of identification with Eduard, the body has passions that reason cannot grasp. The hand held by his father is transformed into the "arm in arm" with his friend and eventually with Martha, suggesting that their romance was infiltrated by a model fundamentally based on same-sex desire and friendship. This later repeated with Breuer, another paternal and friendly figure: in 1883, Freud wrote to Martha that they had ran into each other and decided to go "arm in arm" toward the Karl Theatre to catch up (Ibid., p. 72). The image of hands returns in his love language: it is right for two people to have joined hands for life in love and friendship; without her, he would have thrown up his arms, but with her he wanted to experience life's happiness to share and enjoy it together.

Love and friendship are again mixed together. Like with Eduard, Freud threatened Martha he would stop writing if she did not respond. Silence, he argued, led to false opinions and even to estrangement. "Nor shall I always be very affectionate, sometimes I will be serious and outspoken, as is only right between friends and as friendship demands" (p. 29). He would treat her according to her worth and merit, contrary to those who would spoil her as a charming toy. Since entering into their alliance, they had to change slightly to love each other, he wrote. Yet he himself nevertheless showed little inclination to change, when he wrote that she saw the world in the same way he did. He was also profoundly hurt when she initially refused to give up her friendship with Fritz Wahle. "[E]ven for a beloved girl there is still one further step up: to that of a friend" (p. 30). For Freud, this was associated with the idea of loving the other as an equal, not having to hide the truth from them as one would from a child. Friendship was set up as the ideal model for any relationship, more valuable than even a romantic connection. "Please accept the hand which I hold out to you in fondest affection and confidence and do with me as I am doing with you" (Ibid.), he suggested.

Given the little professional success he had gained so far, especially after his failed attempt at making a discovery in his research on cocaine, he confided in her his temptation to forget medicine and "lead a regular gypsy life" (p. 53). His health concerns became more precise. He had struggled so much over the previous two years (1881 and 1882) that he needed all the joy and happiness brought to him by Martha to remain well. He felt "like a clock that hasn't been repaired for a long time, dusty in every joint" (Ibid.). Since obtaining her, he had taken on a greater importance, even for himself; he was therefore more concerned with his health and did not want to overwork himself. He would prefer to renounce his ambitions, attract less attention and have less success rather than endanger his nervous system, even if it meant to know less about it. When trying to make their separation less painful by daydreaming about their life once reunited, he spoke about Martha's eyes, the part standing for the whole, to compensate him for this long period of waiting. He wanted her to be not just the housekeeper and the cook, but "a precious friend and a cherished sweetheart as well" (p. 105). Even before his crucial encounter with Fliess, bisexuality therefore already played a central role in Freud's conception of any important relationship.

3.18   Writing a story for his golden beloved

Just like in his correspondence with Eduard, Freud included a fictional story in his letters, inspired by *Nathan the Wise*, a 18th-century drama by the German play-wright Gotthold Ephraim Lessing. In another example of idealising great literary figures, Freud mentioned Lessing in another letter, after having accidentally come across his statue in Hamburg. He spoke about him as someone who had both recent and ancient rights over him, who could guide rather than separate everyone on this earth. He thought of the relief he had felt on reading a page from Lessing and placed Martha, in a remnant of faith, under the great man's protection.

In the fantasy scenario based on Lessing's play, elements of reality – such as concerning Martha's father – combined with fiction, setting up a dialogue between him and an old Jewish man with a shaggy beard, who was none other than Martha's grandfather. The father-son relationship played a significant role, against the contrast between the Jewish religion and Catholicism. Simply put, Freud evoked two conceptions of pleasure: the Jew states that nine days before the Fast Day, you must deny yourself every pleasure. He adds that he belongs to a group of men of the old school, who adhere to their religion without cutting themselves off from life. They owe their education to one single man, a certain Isaac Bernays, Martha's grandfather, whom Freud made the head of the Jewish community. "Me? I grew up with the sons", he continues, of whom there were three, including Jacob Bernays, Professor of Classical Philology and Martha's uncle. The father, a linguist, was an interpreter of the Scriptures; all his children were very talented, he adds.

The description of the three sons, following the same generational line as Freud, alludes to three images of Freud himself, especially apropos the youngest son. The first son chooses to study languages, to which he devotes his scientific career; the second is teaching the subtleties and the wisdom that the great poets and teachers put into their writings. The third son is serious, taciturn, but understands life on a deeper level than science and art are able to. He is above all a human being and creates new treasures rather than interpreting old ones. "Glory to the memory of him who presented me with my Marty!" Freud delights, his revolutionary tendencies taking a precise inflection here: standing with the generation of fathers rather than sons and questioning the interpretations of the elders, including in the realm of science. Already since adolescence, the desire to overturn the acquired and transmitted knowledge was the aim of the future creator of psychoanalysis.

Although this is purely a personal fantasy, I should point out that in French the term *trésor* [treasure] ends with the "*or*" [gold] of Freud's childhood nickname – the "Golden Sigi". Many combinations with the precious metal emerge – in his letters and also his later references to Midas, or thinking of the "pure gold" of psychoanalysis.

With Martha, we have already seen that during one of his low moods, he wrote he no longer felt the "magic of gold" (p. 57). He also told her what he had been working on. Still at Brücke's laboratory, he explained that it was him who had been the most successful at silvering and gilding of the sliced segments of the brain to obtain clearer images of its fibres or cells. It was a question of technical tricks, he told her. He had shown his teacher his gildings; the latter said that gold had not been known to be much use for this purpose and might yet make him famous (p. 73). Again, gold and a wish for fame were linked; the precious metal, symbol of Freud's value or, on the contrary, his feelings of inferiority, now returned to give value to Martha. Freud told his fiancée jokingly that the girls engaged to Dozents should wear golden bracelets to distinguish them from the fiancées of ordinary doctors. Gold indeed symbolised the exceptionality Freud had attributed to himself since childhood and which he now extended to Martha. Should he make any discoveries in the next three months, she would have the golden snake promised to her in Nothnagel's time.

Let's return to the structure of the novel written by the amorous young man. In the story, Freud introduces a teacher who is not an ascetic, contrary to the group of the old Jewish man who in their fictional dialogue has previously told him, "The Jew . . . is the finest flower of mankind, and is made for enjoyment. Jews despise anyone who lacks the ability to enjoy" (Ibid, p. 21). This reminded Freud that while drunk, Eli had once disclosed his life philosophy in honour of the Jew: *Homo sum*. He remembered that the law commanded every Jewish person to appreciate even the smallest enjoyment, to bless each fruit that makes him aware of his attachment to this beautiful world in which it is grown. The Jew is made for joy and joy for the Jew, he argued. He thought of their couple with regards to this meaningful Judaism full of joie de vivre for their future home. The euphoria of his encounter with Martha was patent: the psycho-sexual misery was replaced by a hope for a joyful life where pleasures would be supported by religion, contrary to Freud's later belief that it was the source of many neuroses.

For him, pleasure derived from his library and his familiar lamp. Also, he imagined, there would be objects in the house kept by Martha, a love for beautiful things, fondly remembered friends, old cities they have visited or hours they would like to relive – silent friends attesting to their noble feelings. The long-distance relationship with Martha provoked new daydreams about this future, especially their future day-to-day lives.

3.19   The repression of adolescence and its Oedipal scars

In the course of their courtship, certain character traits of Freud's adolescence were transformed or faded. These changes were often linked to a process of repression more profound than it might initially appear. Yet when he spoke about the effects of meeting Martha, this did not seem to be the case:

> I am afraid I do have a tendency toward tyranny, as someone recently told me, and added to this is the fact that I am all too gay nowadays; I let myself go in a kind of youthful high spirits of immaturity, which used to be quite alien to me.
>
> (p. 43)

Despite the distance between them, their relationship allowed him to experience a part of his adolescence he had previously repressed too strongly to actually live it. At this moment of openness and hope brought by their romantic encounter, he was able to pick up the thread, hence his sense that the psychic work of his youth was far from done.

Despite the appearances and Freud's authoritarian proclivities, I tend to agree with the view of Grubrich-Simitis and Lortholary (2012), who argue that the beginnings of their romance were indeed tyrannical, although its conclusion was peaceful. This did not prevent Freud from retaining, for example, his tendency to hate certain people for purely intellectual reasons, even if the simple-minded was fundamentally a good person, and continue to judge others on their intelligence, which remained his measure for both men and women.

Some transformations were obvious on a number of occasions. In one letter, he wrote that his search for accolades was becoming too exhausting and he would prefer to do something useful and enjoy their life together. We have already seen this reversal of perspective as to the importance of love, compared to focusing solely on his glorious destiny. However, his following words are marked by a repression of his ambitious and passionate letters to Eduard: he explained to his fiancée that at the beginning of his studies, he was not particularly ambitious. He was seeking in science the satisfaction of the effort of searching and the moment of discovery (p. 57) – quite contrary to his wish to preserve, in the case of a discovery, the eternal glory of the idea. "I don't think I am ambitious, although not exactly unsusceptible to recognition" (p. 158), he also wrote, a formulation echoing more of a compromise formation. Later in his autobiography, when speaking about his relationship with certain philosophers, especially Schopenhauer and Nietzsche, Freud transformed this conflict by subordinating his ambitions to his desire for knowledge: "I was less concerned with the question of priority than with keeping my mind unembarrassed."

During his evolving relationship with Martha, these factors also encouraged another, second wave of repression – after latency – specific to the emotional stabilisation of post-adolescent life. The time when the challenges of separation disturbed "the equilibrium of a profoundly exalted sensibility" (Grubrich-Simitis, Lortholary, 2012, p. 786) had passed, giving way to a more constant regulation of conflicts. His happiness now depended more on his relationship with Martha and on regular and peaceful work. Previously, love and creative passion were opposites; now passion for science could exist alongside a tranquil love life. Martha would become the pillar of this psychic reorganisation, managing domestic life and supporting Freud's creativity. This potential stabilisation was accompanied by alternating between passivity and activity. We have seen the active dimension in Freud's tyrannical requests and his need to control the love-object. For instance, after one of their disagreements he promised Martha that when they would see each other again, he would be her strict but loving and caring master. However, he also declared himself prepared to be ruled by his "princess", and argued that one willingly let oneself be dominated by the person one loved (Freud, 1873–1939, p. 51).

In his friendships, the model of his infantile-adolescent neurosis remained unchanged with respect to the figure of the "frenemy". At the same time, he seemed less defended and more in touch with his feelings. He wrote about a friend with whom he liked to complain about the absurdity of the world. His friend read a few lines from Goethe to him, which provoked such intense emotion and had more meaning for Freud than for his friend, "that I had to run away in order not to betray myself and to be alone with my thoughts". His upset made him unable to work that day. While as a teenager his passion for books and knowledge was paramount, as a young adult he became more flexible. Being moved by Goethe's lines which likely recalled a memory, he temporarily let himself drop work in order to listen to himself and react in a way more in touch with what he was feeling (go out to meet with another friend).

About his friendships, he wrote:

Contact with friends holds for me nowadays a special charm – the seriousness of life seems to have disclosed itself to us almost simultaneously; what in the beginning seemed to us dear and desirable, but easily accessible, has now withdrawn into the far distance although still remaining dear.

(Freud, 1873–1939, p. 26)

This suggests that the desires of adolescence were replaced by new aims, but also that adolescence now belonged to the sphere of memory and its reconstructions.

Another clue lies in Freud's use of the term "scar", painting a picture of the wounds of adolescence. The term later returned when he spoke about the scars left behind by the Oedipus complex in his analysis of his daughter Anna (Houssier, 2010). In a letter to Breuer, Freud wrote that for many people, their mental epidermis would have been torn open by the traumatic events of his life, but he was hoping for a "solid layer of scars" (Freud, 1873–1939, p. 115). He was still more direct when speaking about his encounter with Martha: "And since then I too have become another person, many wounds that went deeper than you knew have been closed, and I feel within me a gaiety and a self-confidence which for a whole year had been unknown to me." Somewhat later, he wrote that he had undergone a more profound change than he had thought. It was then that he realised that he had never really been young, but falling in love gave him a new youthful élan. Two weeks away from seeing his fiancée, he was daydreaming about Martha's kisses quenching his thirst, about leading "a very different life that will make both of us whole and young again" (p. 124). This time, the daydream seemed less conflict-ridden, with a certain correction of the past – a different kind of youth than his own, similarly to his later treatment of his memory of Gisela (Freud, 1899).

In the same way, he became equal to his teachers. Looking back, he spoke about a time of doing research and dreaming about a sweet girl who would become everything to him, whom he had now managed to win. He considered that he had made a lot of progress since that time. The men previously admired by him from afar as inaccessible were now speaking to him on equal terms and showed him their friendship (Freud, 1873–1939, p. 74). He felt safe from what was the worst fate for him – solitude. He had remained in good health and had done nothing dishonourable. However, he could now also obtain what he needed – a sign of the independence he had long searched for.

3.20   "Life is hard, but I am drugging myself in work"

In a letter, he wrote about sorting out his patient observations and starting to study a nervous case: "[T]hus begins a new era!" he exclaimed. However, to his great frustration, some of his colleagues too were beginning to focus on the question of the neuroses. For several days, he was thus in low spirits, exasperated by the slightest irritation, including the infrequency of Martha's letters. Professional competition and distance from his beloved seem interlinked. Once his mood improved, he wrote that he had again found his zest for work and that his impatience will one day probably make him explode (Freud, 1873–1939, p. 93). He had seen a neurotic patient, Martha's compatriot, whose case he might like to publish one day.

His work was not just a source of frustrations; he also wrote that "in any case, I am learning a lot, including about myself", concluding the letter by a request that Martha too should not keep her thoughts to herself. When moralism and jealousy did not threaten to destroy everything in their way, introspection and free-association remained a constant in Freud's mind. In November 1882, when he wrote that "my little girl tells me every thought that flutters in her little head", he insisted that nothing should be hidden or effaced, i.e., censured. The central idea he was developing was thus "bringing truth to light". Once again, he was calling for introspection and deep self-exploration as a disposition common to both of them, a romantic ideal already present in his relationship with Eduard.

In other ways too, he felt liberated: he was overjoyed at having overcome his former timidity and delivered a triumphant lecture before the severe Meynert, several psychiatrists and colleagues (p. 98). In terms of his finances, the generosity of friends such as Paneth and his fiancée gave him hope to be able to marry Martha. Paneth offered him an unsolicited loan of fifteen hundred gulden; he could now really plan their marriage, and after the idea of moving to Manchester, he was now thinking about them emigrating to America. He was thrilled by the idea of at last being able to work and earn enough to no longer have to feel ashamed.

Freud proposed to his fiancée even though reason should have told her to say no, he wrote, but also that with her he finally found confidence in himself. He now wanted to obtain an official position in the field of paediatric nervous diseases. To love and to work – at last, the two conditions were fulfilled to begin his adult life.

Chapter 4

Retroactive explorations

Freud and his sons

Our study of Freud's correspondence has shown us his quasi-vital need to confide in a person fulfilling the function of a double, correlated with certain rivalrous tensions regarding the degree of intelligence of each of these interlocutors, both men and women. His friendship with Eduard Silberstein was a kind of prototype, in which the key psychic challenges of this relationship to a double became condensed. Later in his life, a new element in his correspondence no longer had to do with a desire for a close relationship but rather its opposite, a fear of meeting one's double. This question, already present in Freud's teenage years, returned especially with Arthur Schnitzler. Although this is by far not an exhaustive picture, I have chosen to present two other examples of relational proximity: Freud's relationship with his sons and with Sándor Ferenczi, to illustrate two kinds of connections that in Freud's adult life again brought to surface some of the complex aspects of his adolescence.

4.1 A looming shadow

We have previously explored what some have called the psychic twinship between Freud and Silberstein. The narcissistic intensity of this relationship cannot be reduced to the "frenemy" figure of Freud's childhood; the ambivalence towards his cousin John, underpinned by sexual rivalry, can also be understood as a representation of Freud's bisexual identification, using conflict to fend off an invasive and incestuous proximity. We can "hear" the narcissistic relationship between Freud and his double John when in the context of dream analysis the former talks about an incident, in which his father asked him why he had hit his cousin. Freud justified himself by saying that he only hit him after he had been hit. This infantile trace presents a point of articulation with those Freud considered as complementary to himself, such as Eduard and Martha. It creates a line of continuity between questions of narcissistic differentiation: Freud's conflictual stance towards his loved ones would thus also reflect a need for differentiation essential to a sense of the self (Houssier, 2018b). The narcissistic and identity questions as well as the work of subjectivation characteristic of adolescence are paradigmatic of this fundamental need; for Freud, the need to separate oneself and grasp one's sense of identity came

DOI: 10.4324/9781003437062-5

after a period of confounding himself with the object, echoing the torments of the mother-baby relationship.

It was not accidental that the function of the double reappeared at the turn of the century, during the most fertile period of his return to his adolescence. The first double after Silverstein was Wilhelmina Fliess. Vermorel (2018) has commented on their joint photograph as a portrait of a narcissistic transference, where the other is a narcissistically invested object, positioned between a merging with the object, which is nevertheless seen as distinct, and the projective identification of a grandiose self. The negative component of the relationship, more clearly apparent with Fliess than with Silberstein, gave Freud the opportunity and the urgency to break off their connection, which was of course very painful. For Freud, the question was not of a transference to a third person (Ibid, p. 62) but rather to a common space of elaboration, which was also a source of confusion, between persecution and an encounter with otherness.

4.1.1   Phobia of the double

In 1906, two years after visiting the Acropolis with his brother, Freud wrote to Arthur Schnitzler, a writer also living in Vienna, to whom he expressed his sense of the conformity of their views. He used a reference to his clinical work with a young girl, Dora, to show their common ground:

> For many years I have been conscious of the far-reaching conformity existing between your opinions and mine on many psychological and erotic problems; and recently I even found the courage expressly to emphasize this conformity ("Fragment of an Analysis of a Case of Hysteria," 1905). I have often asked myself in astonishment how you came by this or that piece of secret knowledge which I had acquired by a painstaking investigation of the subject, and I finally came to the point of envying the author whom hitherto I had admired.
>
> (Freud, 1873–1939, p. 251)

Flattered by having been cited by the admired writer, Freud added other narcissistic qualities to their relationship: pride and honour. The letters stopped there and the two never ended up meeting; however, Freud's publications kept him in contact with the literary world and their correspondence resumed some sixteen years later, on 14th May 1922, on the occasion of Schnitzler's sixtieth birthday. Freud was then sixty-six years old. On this occasion, Freud confided in him as if by extending his self-analysis, again trying to find a close reciprocal relationship without outside interference:

> But I will make a confession which for my sake I must ask you to keep to yourself and share with neither friends nor strangers. I have tormented myself with the question why in all these years I have never attempted to make your acquaintance and to have a talk with you?

Fabre (2014) points out the sense of unease marked by the repetition of "confession" in this letter. Freud continues:

> The answer contains the confession which strikes me as too intimate. I think I have avoided you from a kind of reluctance to meet my double. . . . Whenever I get deeply absorbed in your beautiful creations I invariably seem to find beneath their poetic surface the very presuppositions, interests, and conclusions which I know to be my own.
>
> (Freud, 1873–1939, p. 339)

Freud and Schnitzler shared a "preoccupation with the truths of the unconscious", this time adding a resonance with the text on the *Uncanny* (Freud, 1919a):

> [A]ll this moves me with an uncanny feeling of familiarity. . . . So I have formed the impression that you know through intuition – or rather from detailed self-observation – everything that I have discovered by laborious work on other people. Indeed, I believe that fundamentally your nature is that of an explorer of psychological depths.
>
> (p. 339–40)

Note that J. Popper-Lynkeus also showed a profound understanding of dreams; in his case too, Freud (1932) made sure to explain that they had never actually met.

As he described in his original article (Freud, 1919a), being confronted with a different image of oneself can trigger an anxiety, a fear of meeting one's double. Contrary to Romain Rolland and a number of others considered acceptable doubles of Fliess (Vermorel, 2018), the absence of geographical distance made the sense of threat of the double's presence even more intense. Here again, was it not the case that physical distance was seen as protective, as suggested by Freud's correspondence with Silberstein and with Martha Bernays? The pain of separation clashed against the phobia of too much closeness, reminding us of Freud's argument about two twin brothers (1920): in order not to be mistaken with the other during the sexual act, one of the brothers becomes homosexual to guarantee their distinction. This confusing proximity comes alongside a need for substitution, for a change of identity, as shown by Freud's correspondence with the writers and scientists he admired. Hence the idea that both Silberstein and Fliess were not simply alter egos. Each of them fantasmatically embodied a patient for Freud and, on the other hand, an analyst. The feminine position, both desired and rejected by Freud, should therefore be understood as a desire to be fecundated intellectually by the alter ego's thought (Vermorel, 2018).

When he was researching the motif of the double, Freud (1919a) highlighted a key metapsychological aspect of this confusion by proximity: isn't this exchange of the foreign ego for one's own at work in all twin relationships? Fabre (2014) emphasises the function, for the ageing and cancer-ridden Freud, of the double as a defence against the ego's disappearance. The author also cites a series of doubles, going back as far as Freud's dead brother Julius, to formulate a hypothesis around his fear of death, namely that the malevolent and feared double exerted a pull towards death, while at the same time mobilising a massive amount of survivor's guilt. This hypothesis can be sustained if we link it to maternal depression rather than Freud's hypothetical memory traces. Freud's fascination with his early memories discovered in self-analysis had its negated equivalent, namely the way in which this early infantile material was recomposed during adolescence. The need for a double necessarily also recalls the double maternal figure of Freud's childhood – his mother and his nanny – a double later restored in Freud's marriage through the two sisters, Martha and Minna Bernays, and later in the following generation thanks to the couple of Anna Freud and Dorothy Burlingham (Houssier, 2010) or even Anna Freud and Melanie Klein.

Both Vermorel and Fabre nevertheless forget one of the paradigmatic doubles in Freud's life, Eduard Silberstein. With him, Freud created a double relationship allowing him to live, a permanent support helping him cope with the struggles of his adolescent years. The fact that he was able to bear their ultimate separation was due to his concurrent massive investment of his first professional steps and later his encounter with Martha Bernays.

4.1.2   Between confusion and differentiation

If we return to his friendship with Eduard, we will remember, for example, the fantasy of the shared house (Houssier, 2018a). Freud was looking for a double, hence his at times acerbic remarks when Eduard was too slow to respond to his letters. This search for a double then continued with Martha and later with Fliess, without really distinguishing between friendship and love, which often seem as interlinked. Kanzer (1976) highlights the importance of literary doubles in Freud's life, especially Goethe and Cervantes; the latter created a first couple, Cipion and Berganza, before Freud discovered *Don Quixote* and the story of the inseparable duo of the idealist knight and his servant Sancho Panza.

We can add to this the episode of Gisela and her mother, experienced as a double ideal of his own mother, who herself had a double in Freud's nanny. When Freud (1899) returned to this story, he invented a patient as a double of himself, as a form of protection while tackling the story of his own youth.

His dreams also appear permeated by this question; without going into the details of his dream about his patient Irma, probably Anna Hammerschlag (Anzieu, 1989), let us simply identify some of its elements that play on the theme of the double. His colleague, nicknamed Léopold, in fact the paediatrician Ludwig Rosenberg, who was Freud's assistant at Dr Kassowitz's children's clinic, perceives a "dull area" on the left side of the examined patient's body. In Freud's dream, he notices this "just as [Léopold] did" (Freud, 1900, p. 113), emphasising the image of a sensory double founded on an identity of perception and the corporeality of sensations. This is a bisexual identification; in his patient's affliction, Freud recognises his own rheumatism in the left shoulder. He adds: " 'I noticed this, just as he did. . . .' I noticed it in my own body that is" (p. 113). This flexibility of identification is made possible by replacing his patient with a friend of hers; this time what is at stake is a sexual desire rather than a narcissistic search. "And how strangely, I thought to myself, a dream like this is put together! The other woman, whom I had as a patient in the dream instead of Irma, was also a young widow" (p. 117).

Since his adolescence, Freud experienced intense conflict: on the one hand, he was driven by a fantasy of finding a guarantee, using these twin-like relationships as a protection against abandonment and loss, but also as a narcissistic refuge for his sexual desires. Certain objectal aspects notwithstanding, the tendency was therefore towards a non-differentiation between himself and the other. His assertion that he had succeeded where the paranoiac fails can be understood in another way: where Fliess failed to successfully separate from Freud and was invaded, at the end of their relationship, by a paranoiac conviction that Freud was trying to kill him, the latter had arguably succeeded to free himself of this bond, despite the particularly intense suffering caused by their separation. In general, Freud's twin-like relationships did not end well, hence his cautiousness towards meeting people he admired and considered as doubles. On the other hand, his great need for self-affirmation, compensating for his lack of confidence, was also a constant of his youth, setting up an articulation between a confusion with a passionately invested alter ego and a process of subjective differentiation. We should add that the problem of idea theft that, following his relationship with Fliess, later poisoned the entire psychoanalytic movement also resonates with the question of the double. In this kind of merging of identifications, how do we know where ideas come from? We also notice a similar difficulty when Freud questions his own originality by exploring cryptomnesia (Houssier, 2018a). In this case, his doubles are the literary or scientific idols of his teenage years.

This difficulty continued, especially in Freud's relationships with certain of his disciples and friends who shared his ideal of the psychoanalytical cause. Amongst the most significant elements of the aftermath of his adolescence, his relationship with his own sons also emerged as a source of conflict. This time, his dreams referred to his sons' youth, suggesting that their own adolescence had an impact at a time of Freud's preoccupations with his own ageing.

4.2   Gold and copper of ambivalence

The fact that Freud channelled a part of his own neurosis into his theory does not in itself make him exceptional. His method, using self-analysis, was nevertheless just as singular as it was productive, despite its personal limitations, of which he soon became aware. The two volumes I have written about his adolescence rely largely on the *Interpretation of Dreams* (Freud, 1900), a work whose autobiographical tones are well known. The few dream extracts I have presented are, of course, far from exhaustive as to the breath of possible reinterpretations of the topic. The last theme among Freud's dream investigations I will address combines the present and the past based on the adolescence of his own sons.

4.2.1 A royal road

Freud's dream book was written between 1895 and 1899, at a time when Freud reached the age of 40. This was a crucial period in his life, a time when he had gained enough distance from his youthful emotions to try and elaborate some of their sharp edges, while also still connected to the traces of their conflicts. In April 1896, he wrote to Fliess: "As a young man my only longing was for philosophical knowledge, and now that I am changing over from medicine to psychology I am in the process of fulfilling this wish" (Freud, 1873–1939, p. 231).

The sentence is an accurate summary of his journey: an adolescent who tried to escape his libidinal conflicts through intellectualisation slowly became a young man fighting against his speculative tendencies through his studies and a rationalising profession, before psychology brought these two sides of his psychic functioning together in a kind of ego-syntonic synthesis.

In his memories and other associations linked to his self-analysis, which were often included in his letters to Fliess, the questions of the secret and confidentiality were still very present, just like in his letters to Silberstein. He tried to justify himself methodologically, only to at last decide that in the interest of science, he was going to include personal material in his book on dreams, while making it clear that he would regularly censor things not essential to the elucidation of the given theoretical concept. Rather than guilt, it was the shame of exhibiting his private life that bothered him. However, shame later became a recurrent theme in his clinical accounts and in the various biographical elements included in the *Interpretation of Dreams*, as an offspring of the agency most definitely formed during adolescence: the ego ideal (Houssier, 2010), the contingencies of which we followed in the course of Freud's younger years.

When it came to his personal life, he felt there was a conflict between modesty and demonstration. This is what he wrote: "There is some natural hesitation about revealing so many intimate facts about one's mental life; nor can there be any guarantee against misinterpretation by strangers" (Freud, 1900, p. 105). The persecutory tone of his words is related to the irrational fear of revealing something intimate, which returned obsessively in his correspondence with Silberstein. Shame was especially present in all of his precautions, injunctions or implorations that punctuated Freud's letters to Eduard.

In his work, he cited Delboeuf, for whom

"Every psychologist is under an obligation to confess even his own weaknesses, if he thinks that it may throw light upon some obscure problem." And it is safe to assume that my readers too will very soon find their initial interest in the indiscretions which I am bound to make replaced by an absorbing immersion in the psychological problems upon which they throw light.

(Ibid., p. 105, n1)

Even though he sounds authentic, Freud would always try to justify himself when it came to the fantasies of self-exposure implied in revealing what he experienced as a weakness, and which threatened to humiliate him in the eyes of others. At the beginning of the century, his dreams of nakedness, which he saw as typical, revealed to Freud his exhibitionist tendencies which emerged from his adolescent years. These dreams later faded away, at a time when his own sons reached adolescence (Blum, 2001).

4.2.2   Protection and envy: Freud's sons

Let us return one more time to some of Freud's reminiscences. In an addition dating from 1919, Freud, then aged sixty-three, provided an account of a dream in which his oldest son has left to fight in the war. One of the central associations of the dream referred to a childhood memory which Freud situated between the ages of two and three: he climbed on a stool in a store-closet, trying to reach some delicacy on a cupboard or a table. He fell and the corner of the stool hurt his lower jaw. "I might easily, I reflected, have knocked out all my teeth," he added. (Freud, 1900, p. 560). He continued:

> The recollection was accompanied by an admonitory thought: "that serves you right"; and this seemed as though it was a hostile impulse aimed at the gallant soldier. Deeper analysis at last enabled me to discover what the concealed impulse was which might have found satisfaction in the dreaded accident to my son: it was the envy which is felt for the young by those who have grown old, but which they believe they have completely stifled. And there can be no question that it was precisely the strength of the painful emotion which would have arisen if such a misfortune had really happened that caused that emotion to seek out a repressed wish-fulfilment of this kind.
>
> (Ibid.)

The first French translation speaks simply about

> the jealousy for the young, which I thought I had completely stifled and . . . when a misfortune of this kind arrives, the intensity of the pain, which is looking for a relief, goes as far as to trigger these repressed wishes in our unconscious.

This childhood memory had to do with the age of his son, who had now become a young man, reversing the death wish on the generational level by turning it into envy and jealousy. The youth perceived by those who feel their death coming mobilises infanticidal wishes, which resonate with parricides desires (Houssier, 2013). As for the teeth that Freud might have knocked out as a child, we may note that the breaking of a tooth in a dream can be interpreted in multiple ways. Freud made it at first into a symbol of castration; later, although he retained this initial idea, he associated it with a puberty ritual in the so-called primitive societies, a rite of passage associated with the boy's becoming part of the community as a pubescent and later as a young man (Freud, 1913).

Freud's preoccupation at the time had to do with his relationship to death. He confided in Fliess that he was worried he would not live over the age of fifty-one, according to a magical theory which combined Fliess' ideas about periodicity and a superstition linked to Jacob Freud's sexual history (Anzieu, 1989). This fear of death did not pertain to his children's future in general but specifically to their adolescence. In a passage devoted to the dreamer's egotism, Freud thus wrote, analysing a dream featuring his friend Otto, who was also his children's doctor: "But my friend Otto was the person whom I had asked to watch over my children's physical education, *especially* at the age of puberty . . ., in case anything happened to me" (Freud, 1900, p. 270, my emphasis). Through a series of associations, he arrived at the following interpretation: "So once again I was wanting to be a Professor! Indeed the words 'late in life' were themselves a wish-fulfilment; for they implied that I should live long enough to see my boys through the age of puberty myself" (p. 271). We note that here again, there is no ambiguity as to the possible confusion between puberty and adolescence: seeing his sons through the age of puberty includes the entire trajectory of adolescence rather than just a physiological event. At the same time, it is difficult not to see this dream interpretation as connected to Freud's identification with his sons – rather than his daughters – underpinned by the idea that they would be going through adolescence alone, without support, given Freud's own intense experiences of solitude, as he described them in particular to his fiancée. The idea that seems to unfold in the dream would thus involve a latent thought: "Perhaps I can help them avoid what I myself had to go through in such a painful way." While in his correspondence with Fliess, Freud regularly shared his concerns for the health of his children, both sons and daughters, linked to all the somatic problems they experienced, his dream takes a different turn.

After highlighting that he had entrusted the health of his pubescent children to his friend Otto, he explains that his dream indicates that in reality he could not have expected much bodily rescue from his friend, who in the dream seemed to be suffering from morbid symptoms. The deep-seated wish of the dream was therefore to live long enough – to exceed the prediction of fifty-one years – in order to protect his sons by watching over their adolescence. Here too, adolescence was designated as a source of problems to be monitored, implicitly accusing Freud's own father of not having been supportive enough. Jacob in fact proved to be lacking equally by failing to provide the desired sexual enlightenment at a time of Freud's "pubertal curiosity" (Freud, 1905b) and in the professional domain. We can assume that Freud's father was held responsible for many of the torments borne by young Freud's inner conflicts, but also that ambivalence was strong in their relationship. This is also the idea of the dream: taking the place of a doctor who is well respected but turns out to be unreliable, probably representing the figure of Jacob Freud.

We could continue with a scene that followed Freud's relationship with Fliess and also greatly resonated with Ferenczi, to which I will return later. After the disappointment with Jung and his supposedly "juvenile" attitude (Freud, 1910a), Freud gradually became invested in Ferenczi as his favourite son. However, what do we see when we look at their relationship more closely?

In a letter to Ferenczi from 6th October 1910, Freud wrote that he had not overcome his countertransference in the following sense: the transference was impossible to work through, both with Ferenczi and with his own three sons, "because I like them and I feel sorry for them in the process" (Freud, Ferenczi, 1908–1914, p. 221). He went on to say that he no longer needed the full opening of his personality that had consisted in confiding intimately in another person, as he had done with Fliess. A part of his homosexual investment had been withdrawn and used for the enlargement of his own ego, resulting in the well-known declaration: "I have succeeded where the paranoiac fails" (Idem.). His relationship with Fliess was permeated by a number of elements related to adolescence, especially during their period of conflict (Houssier, 2016).[1]

4.3   Adolescence in Freud's relationship with Ferenczi

The relationship between Freud and Ferenczi has already been commented on abundantly, especially as part of the effort trying to rehabilitate the latter's work. These authors have shown a continuity of the link tinged with homosexual transference between Freud and Fliess, and later between Freud and Ferenczi. For Jones (1958), the bond with Ferenczi was the most important relationship that Freud created in his late years. If we consider that the connection with Fliess took on the passionate character of Freud's teenage friendship with Eduard Silberstein (Houssier, 2015a), adolescence[2] is indeed represented in the relationship between Freud and Ferenczi, which their correspondence can show more clearly. This homosexual dimension, which included persecutory paranoiac elements, had to do especially with the disturbing feeling of being in the feminine position, i.e., passive, receptive and castrated. After they spent their holidays together in 1910, Freud wrote to Jung that he found Ferenczi too admiring, and thus too passive and feminine like a woman. There was some unruly homosexual feeling at the root of the matter, he also wrote to Jones in 1912, after he had been reminded of Fliess on his visit to Munich. Freud tried to control his passivity, while in 1911 he wrote apropos Schreber that the feminine position would be to have sexual intercourse with a man and identify with the woman's position.

These elements seem significant as to the hypothesis that the Oedipal traces of the father-son relationship, although not exclusive, were also at the heart of the relationship between Freud and Ferenczi. According to Lotto (2001), Freud's friendships with Breuer, Fliess, Adler, Jung, Stekel, Tausk, Rank and Ferenczi followed the same model: love, idealisation, admiration and later anger, hostility and devaluation. Most of the time, they ended in a complete breakdown of the relationship.

4.3.1   The father-son relationship in Freud's theory

Before we examine the complexity of the relationship between the two men, let's briefly return to the turning point of Freud's giving up of his *neurotica*: in abandoning the theory of the generalised sexual abuse of children, Freud turned the tables in two ways at once. The story of a fantasy that later became the Oedipus complex transformed reality from an incestuous enactment into a scenario of desire. The potentially culpable adult was "exonerated" in favour of the child's sexual and murderous wishes. This double turn changed and reoriented the entire Freudian theory: it provoked the construction of a theoretical-mythical line as a displacement of a primarily clinical construction, towards an association anchored between the clinic and mythology, leading to a more structured theorisation. As it was often the case, Freud used culture to support his biographical-theoretical discoveries, in this case refusing to see his father as a perverse seducer. The Oedipus complex found a mythological extension, a kind of doubling, in the story of the primal horde, which again raised the question of an abusive father (Houssier, 2013), while confirming the violence of the adolescent sons towards a parent, the father. Questioning the age of the father's murderers as Freud did, with regards to Oedipus as well as the older brothers of the horde, cannot be simply reduced to an infantile complex; it is also because they have become young men that the sons are able, both physically and psychically, to commit the decisive act. Therefore, were we to know the age of these young men, we would have every interest in exploring another dark continent – that of adolescence – which the organic link between father and son in Freudian theory brings alive. We can argue that the third essay on the theory of sexuality is Freud's key contribution to the transformations of adolescence (Freud, 1905a). However, after this chapter, Freud never wrote anything else on the topic, except for a few occasional comments.

Another connection appears to support this association. To denote both the need to extricate oneself from parental figures of authority in adolescence and the experience of the death of one's father, Freud used the same expression: the greatest pain anyone had to go through in life, which the relationship with Ferenczi precisely illustrated.

4.3.2   Sharing the absent father

As part of their relationship, which combined analysis, friendship and personal issues, Freud remembered a moment of his boyhood when he wrote to Ferenczi on 9th April 1919:

> I received Börne very early as a present, perhaps for my 13th birthday, read him with great enthusiasm, always had a strong recollection of some of these little essays. Naturally not the one on cryptomnesia. When I reread it, I was astonished at how much some things that are in there correspond almost word for word with some things that I have always represented and thought. So he could really be the source of my originality.
>
> (Freud, 1914–1919, p. 344)

Ferenczi's own originality was subject to much criticism, which Ferenczi experienced as the father's wish to exert control over his son.

The figure of the father was evoked regularly for both men, consciously or not. For Freud, we have shown that his bibliophilia originated in a memory of tearing out pages from a book shared with his sister Anna, but also that this memory acted as a screen against another memory of his teenage years (Houssier, 2018a). As if continuing the inner dialogue with a paternal figure, Freud (1900) returned to this autobiographical sequence when he remembered that as a young boy, the debt he accrued with his favourite bookseller provoked his father's negative reaction, while Freud himself saw his passion for books as a better option compared to other forms of enjoyment. Was Freud's ambivalence towards his father not that of an adolescent who, to use his own expression, had sent him to the North Pole dressed in summer clothes (Freud, 1933)? This suggests that one of Ferenczi's criticisms of Freud as a psychoanalyst, namely that his position was too rigidly pedagogical, had intuitively captured what Freud had lacked, namely his father's support in facing his psychosexual anxieties of adolescence.

In these entanglements between private life and analytical work, Ferenczi took on Freud's idea that when sons would leave their adolescent years and become adults, the father only had to die, reminding us of what Freud wrote to Fliess with regards to his fear of dying at the age of fifty-one.

After the death of his daughter Sophie, Freud confided in Ferenczi: "For years I was prepared for the loss of my sons, now comes that of my daughter" (Freud, Ferenczi, 1920–1933, p. 6). The particular investment of his sons and the experience of their adolescence was linked to Freud's institutional preoccupations with the psychoanalytic movement. He thus wrote that in order to live just as much as in order to die, a Jewish father needed to know that the future of his child was secure, evoking Jung's defection but also the hope he had in Ferenczi and the creation of the secret committee (Barande, 1972).

Just to mention a few fragments of Ferenczi's biography. From a large family, Sándor had grown up in a stimulating intellectual environment: his parents, though emotionally very reserved, were freethinkers. Sabourin (2011, p. 27) highlights this reserve when he writes that "physical contacts were greatly limited". Ferenczi himself wrote about his mother's lack of love and excessive severity; his father, of whom he was the favourite, died when he was fifteen, "at a time when he must have needed him the most" (Idem). His father's interests in culture, politics and literature likely had a great influence on young Ferenczi and formed part of his grieving: his father's revolutionary opinions were transmitted in his son's subversive positions. All these factors were present in his transference to Freud, but also in the narcissistic transference between the two of them. Each of them had in fact suffered from having felt deprived of a father who could support and guide them through their younger years, a reliable figure marred by a professional failure in Freud's case or, in the case of Ferenczi, by an absence and an unfinished process of mourning.

4.3.3   *Between rebellion and idealisation*

The first moment of Ferenczi's rebellion occurred during their shared summer holiday in Sicily in 1910, when Freud asked Ferenczi to become his secretary and note down his ideas on paranoia. Later, Ferenczi thanked Freud for having kept his cool while he underwent a period of rebellion against his treatment.

This first moment of uncertainty did not prevent Freud from describing Ferenczi's character as juvenile and immature, but also as someone who promoted young talent. The references to Ferenczi's extended adolescence were nevertheless accompanied by a certain idealisation on Freud's side, when he considered Ferenczi's work as gold (Shur, 1972b) – and we are aware of the resonance of this term for the "Golden Sigi". Freud, for example, cited Ferenczi's work in his additions to the *Interpretation of Dreams*; for example, Ferenczi's observation that the dream productions of the "uninitiated" provided precious clues as to the meaning of typical symbols and dream significations. Even though the word "uninitiated" [*Ahnungslosen* – unaware, clueless] might make us think of children, in the same work Freud interpreted a scene of seduction staged by a young female patient as conditioned by her "uninitiated" character (Houssier, Christaki, 2016).

In the transference with his students, Freud easily interpreted conflicts (with Adler, Hall or Jung) as death-wishes against the father. Regarding institutional matters he wrote to Ferenczi on 3rd April 1910, following the second international congress in Nuremberg: "The infancy of our movement has ended with the Nuremberg Reichstag; that is my impression. I hope that a rich and beautiful youth is now coming" (Freud, Ferenczi, 1908–1914, p. 156). Later, in his letter of 17th October 1912, Freud compared himself to the historical Moses, with a hasty temper and prone to fits of passion. He concluded with what he had previously written to Silberstein: he was a conqueror. He also likened himself to Michelangelo, whom he saw as superhuman, as having successfully struggled with his own passion for the sake of a cause to which he had devoted himself. At this time, the narcissism of petty differences involved a certain degree of reciprocity in how their relationship was described. For Freud, they could both be compared to great men, and this idealisation concealed more aggressive aspects. The father-son transference had not yet reached the critical-murderous zone of adolescence. Quite the contrary: in his letter of 26th December 1912, Ferenczi echoed Freud's double comparison, but only to efface himself in favour of Freud's glory, refusing to take a potentially rivalrous position. Freud was the only one, he wrote, who could do without an analyst; nobody could match the advantage of his fifteen years of experience. This advantage of fifteen years not just resonated with the age at which Ferenczi lost his father, but it also established an age gap, pushing Ferenczi into an infantile position vis-à-vis an honoured and adulated paternal figure. Freud, he added, had been able to master his symptoms; his discoveries had been confirmed clinically and, without a leader, for the first time in the history of humanity, he was able to overcome in himself the resistances that all humanity posed to the results of analysis. In this idolising description, Freud had no need for a guide, contrary to Ferenczi; he was the self-engendered hero consecrated by his students.

Ferenczi therefore pleaded for the following fantasy when he complained of Jung: mutual analysis – a method Ferenczi later adopted himself – promoted by Jung was nonsense. The latter should have respected Freud's rules, which dictated that students had to be treated as patients. In other words, those who did not align with this view were in fact opposed to Freud himself. The relationship to the father was reflected in Ferenczi's theoretical criticism of Jung: he considered him a typical instigator, a founder of religion, who would do away with the father in order to promote the Christian community of brothers. The importance given to the horizontality of fraternal relationships was strictly opposed to Freud's understanding of transference, founded on the rediscovery of a vertical and asymmetrical link characteristic of the parent-child relationship.

4.3.4   "Mired in the juvenile"

Freud was aware of Ferenczi's idealisation, so much so that he tried to prevent its effects when he asked himself why they had not been in conflict, given Freud's reservations towards Ferenczi's theoretical and clinical positions. He attributed this to a certain weakness in himself, adding in the letter of 6th October 1910 that "I am also not that $\psi\alpha$ superman whom we have constructed" (1908–1914, p. 221).

Their conflicts finally broke out around the question of a woman, Gizella Pálos, who shared her given name with the young girl of Freud's teenage infatuation. I will not discuss the entire situation here, as it is very complex, but it is useful to identify certain elements linked to the question of adolescence. For a certain time, Ferenczi had been romantically involved with this older woman and wanted to have children with her. Ferenczi's attraction to her daughter Elma was analysed by Freud as linked to Ferenczi's need for paternity and, on the side of the young woman, to her wish to find a paternal substitute.

Ferenczi wrote to Freud, adding to the picture his unsatisfactory sexual life with "Frau G". Part of this mixture of desires was also his fascination with Elma's "coquetry and ill temper", which for Ferenczi referred to a representation of death which he had, according to Freud, strongly invested during his adolescence (1908–1914, p. 392).

At first, Freud, who was conscious of the transferential character of the situation, held back from giving Ferenczi any explicit advice, even though he did not believe that a marriage with Elma would have been happy and had respect for "Frau G". As he revealed some months after the affair seemed to have come to an end, he had been worried that were he to advise Ferenczi against a marriage with the young girl, Ferenczi might still go ahead with it, following neurotic patterns (Ibid., p. 499). Freud's insistence infantilised Ferenczi, who believed that "Elma served as a rationalization of my tendencies toward independence" (Ibid., p. 515). Freud on the other hand intervened even more actively than before to incite Ferenczi to marry Gizella, which was not without an echo with his own adolescent daydreaming about her namesake.

The Elma-Gizella affair, another mother-daughter duo for Freud, concluded when "Frau G", the maternal figure, took a position in her relationship with Ferenczi. Freud thus occupied the place of a decisive third when Ferenczi asked him to act as an intermediary in proposing to Frau G, which Freud did.

After all these peripeties, Ferenczi finally married Gizella in March 1919. He was then forty-six, while she was fifty-four. The first period of analysis took place in October 1914 and lasted fifteen to twenty days, with two sessions a day. It was suddenly interrupted by Ferenczi's mobilisation, which provoked his frustration and an extension of his self-analysis, finally leading him to conclude: "I – despite my years – have still not reached anything definitive [*das Definitivum*], and I am still deeply mired in the juvenile – not to mention the infantile" (Ibid, p. 40). Once again, we hear the significance of interpretations concerning Ferenczi's adolescence, which circulated between him and his analyst. Analysis transformed a person who had remained childish, i.e., basically carefree, into someone else, who was aware of all his responsibilities, he added (p. 133), a tendency that echoed a young person's feelings of responsibility for his affects and other sexual desires.

In 1919, he added to Freud's attention:

> With the ucs. resentment in my heart, I, as a loyal "son", nevertheless followed all your suggestions, left Elma, again turned to my present wife. . . . I am willing to resume – perhaps, actually – to begin the frank intercourse with you, free from petty sensitivity. It appears that I can be happy in life and content in work only when I can be and remain in good, indeed, in the best relations with you. The realization that in Frau G. I have the best that could befall me – with my constitution –, is the first fruit of my inner reconciliation with you.
>
> (p. 356–7)

At this time, beginning a third tranche of his analysis with Freud, he asked him for three or even four sessions per day, as if animated in the transference by a hunger for a father. Nevertheless, marriage and his active technique gradually led to a distancing between the two colleagues and friends, without immediately bringing about a complete breakdown of their relationship. During the same period, Freud (1920) made progress in his understanding of homosexuality and its over-determination by working on the case of Sidonie Csillag, "the young female homosexual". During this time, he was also analysing his own daughter Anna, who herself suffered from a phobic attitude towards men (Houssier, 2010). Adolescence and homosexuality continued to work between the two men, often unbeknownst to them, while the transference between them gradually took on a more negative tone.

4.3.5   Whose father?

On 27th February 1920, Ferenczi wrote to Groddeck:

> Prof. Freud considered my overall physical symptoms for one to two hours; he persists in his original view that the crux of the matter is my hatred for *him*, because he stormed me (just like her father did . . .) from marrying the younger woman (now my stepdaughter). Hence my murderous intentions towards him which express themselves in nightly scenes (drop in body temperature; gasping

for breath). These symptoms are, furthermore, overdetermined by my memories of watching my parents having intercourse. I must admit it did me good to talk for once to this dearly loved father about my hate feelings.

(Ferenczi, 1921–1933, p. 19)

In the transference, Freud was identified with the dead-killed father of Ferenczi's adolescence as the Oedipal father of his childhood. At this point, the friendship between the two men had entered a zone of turbulence ruled by projection and a generalised confusion, while the question of adolescence continued to preoccupy them both.

In August 1931, Freud (1873–1939, p. 444) wrote to Alexander Lipschutz, a professor of physiology who had previously published a volume entitled *The Law of Follicular Constancy, the Law of Puberty and the Anterior Pituitary Lobe*. Freud responded to his well wishes by saying that he had repeatedly cited his book on the pubertal gland, from which he had learnt a great deal. He was happy to say that he was not one of those opposing psychoanalysis to endocrinology, "as if psychic processes could be explained directly by glandular effects or as if the logic of psychic mechanisms could replace the knowledge of the underlying chemistry".

Ferenczi, on the other hand, was not to be left behind. In 1929, he published an article on the suicide of a nineteen-year-old girl which probably referred to Freud's reproaches regarding Ferenczi's sexual excesses, again restaging the choice of a young woman with the duo Gizella/Elma. According to Prado de Oliveira (2011) it was the memory of this young girl that also haunted Ferenczi. Towards the end of their relationship, when Freud reproached Ferenczi for his "kissing technique", the reason was not simply the kiss stolen by his patient Clara Thompson. This kiss was arguably the manifest content, where the latent memory was the young proletarian. Freud conveyed to his patient and friend that he had been blinded by this beautiful nineteen-year-old and overpowered by a counter-transferential event.

Their last meeting took place in September 1932, on the occasion of the Psychoanalytic Congress in Wiesbaden. After this meeting, Freud wrote a letter on 2nd October, in which he berated Ferenczi for something he had allegedly told Brill, namely that Freud had no more insight than a little boy. He wrote that he had foregone any influence he might still have on Ferenczi's psychoanalytical technique: "I don't any longer believe that you will rectify yourself, the way I rectified myself a generation earlier" (1920–1933, p. 445). He added: "The traumatic effect dissipates in me, I am prepared, and used to it." He felt Ferenczi was inaccessible to doubts and imagined this would lead to a traumatic separation which he himself felt confident to be able to overcome.

The generational conflict centred on the father-son relationship seems to have therefore been confirmed by Freud himself, in a tension where each would struggle, in their fantasy, to be the father of the other. Freud was represented as a little boy, Ferenczi either as a child or an adolescent trying to gain independence and a critical mind. Freud's narcissistic disappointment with his favourite adoptive son was palpable and helps us understand the father-adolescent conflict more generally. By extricating himself from his master's tutelage, Ferenczi committed a symbolic murder, of differentiating himself in order to become a subject in his own right. In using the father-son metaphor to analyse the transference, Freud went where, had there not been the generational gap, he might have wished for a more undifferentiated relationship. In his letter, his disappointment was clear, when pointing out that Ferenczi has been systematically turning away from him due to personal hostility, "So there is nothing left for me but to wish you the best," Freud added, convinced that Ferenczi was inaccessible to any doubts – which we can indeed question. His favourite and tumultuous son's efforts to free himself from his authority forced Freud to painfully revisit the abandonments and ruptures of his own past, leading to a certain bitterness.

4.3.6   The last dialogue: the diagnosis of third puberty

In early 1930, Ferenczi criticised Freud for failing to consider his negative transference, in which he idealised the professor. He wrote that Freud had been his revered teacher and unattainable model, a paternal figure that was too out of reach to help him work through his symbolic murder. Despite his lucidity, he still seemed prey to his conflicts of independence and wished not to depend on Freud's goodwill by overestimating his own significance.

Ferenczi and Freud shared a passion for introspection. In his letter from 15th September 1931, as a way of anchoring his infantile-juvenile position, Ferenczi, after a long hiatus in their relationship, wrote about his states of withdrawal as well as a work of inner and outer purification. He tried to lead himself ad absurdum, to sometimes make mistakes, to progress by trial and error, while hoping to reassure Freud that he was not stepping over the bounds of normality. Two positions were expressed here: the fear of being marginalised, or indeed mad – being abnormal – and the need to try and test in order to work through his own conflicts, i.e., two aspects characteristic of the adolescent process.

Freud's response three days later suggests the following interpretation: the interruption of contact between them meant that Ferenczi was increasingly distancing himself from Freud; he hoped this was not the case, but also accepted it as fate. Like so many other things, he wrote, he knew that he was not personally to blame for it, "in recent times I also preferred no one else to you" (1920–1933, p. 418). He pointed out regretfully, as an expression of inner dissatisfaction, that Ferenczi was trying to advance in directions that Freud considered unfruitful.

> But I have – you, yourself, bear witness to this – always respected your independence and am prepared to wait until you yourself take steps to turn around. With you it could be a new, third puberty, after the completion of which you will probably have reached maturity.
>
> (Ibid.)

This time, Freud bluntly designated the resurgence of an adolescent position that had been left unelaborated, suggesting that the previous inner conflicts were also stemming from this position of second adolescence. This referred to the scenarios of seduction between Ferenczi and certain patients, which Freud had always criticised. We also note that Freud offered a clinical hypothesis, according to which the working through of Ferenczi's adolescent conflicts could lead to a mature position which closely resembled the state of mental pacification worthy of an adult.

Ferenczi responded that in the past his actions occasionally led to excesses. In his answer, he associated adolescence with "excursions into uncertainty" and his experimental empirical side, which had always been of value to him. He suggested something similar as to the diagnosis of third puberty. "Let us assume that the diagnosis is correct: the value of what is created in this condition should for the moment be judged objectively" (p. 419), he wrote, adding that what was unusual or strange could also be of interest, according to Freud's quotation from Schiller on literary creativity, "even if it looks in part to be erroneous or fantastic". In his answer, Freud criticised Ferenczi's excessive sexual gratifications, which he considered inappropriate, using at first the image of the sexual revolution promoted by Ferenczi's active technique.

"There is no revolutionary who is not knocked out of the field by a still more radical one" (p. 422), he added, suggesting that others might go beyond kissing to touching, looking, showing, etc. "and Godfather Ferenczi, looking at the busy scenery that he has created, will possibly say to himself: Perhaps I should have stopped in my technique of maternal tenderness before the kiss" (Ibid.). Freud alluded to the fact that Ferenczi had at first enthusiastically promoted his active technique, before he decided to considerably limit its use.

Freud worried that the kissing technique would lead to a rise in the calumnious resistances to analysis; he criticised his former student for having played the role of the tender mother with others and perhaps with himself as well.

And then you should hear the warning from the brutal fatherly side that – to the best of my recollection – the inclination toward sexual games [*Spielerei*] with patients was not alien to you in pre-analytic times, so that one could put the new technique into context with the old misdemeanour. Hence I spoke in an earlier letter about a new puberty in you, a Johannis impulse, and now you have forced me to be unambiguously clear.

(p. 423)

He did not expect to make an impression of Ferenczi, as the basis for that was now missing from their relationship. "The need for defiant self-assertion seems to me to be more powerful in you than you recognize. But at least I have done my part; I have acted true to my father role. Now carry on" (Ibid.). This raises the question: to what father or which image of the father is Freud faithful to here? To the father of conjugal fidelity?

Ferenczi answered that the idea of making his technique public led Freud to make contradictory statements, but this was not the most important thing, now that he had taken the time to calm down and could give a more measured answer. "I consider your fear that I will turn into another Stekel unfounded", he wrote

(p. 424). After the second puberty emerged the image of a second Steckel, hated by Freud for his tactlessness and indecency. Here, just like in the case of Jung and some others, adolescence was perceived as the source of neurotic "demoniacal" impulses, which in Ferenczi's case were associated with excessive sexual freedom. At first, Freud suggested that it would be beneficial to work through this third puberty, before speaking more abruptly about the idea of extinguishing or suppressing it. No doubt this double movement was connected to Freud's ambivalence towards his own adolescence, which he considered as an opportunity of working through as well as an inner enemy to be repressed.

4.3.7   *Ferenczi's intuition: going through a storm*

Let us dwell a bit longer on Ferenczi's answer. He put himself on equal footing with Freud, speaking to him as to an equal, disregarding their age difference. " 'Youthful sins', misdemeanours, when they have been overcome and analytically worked through, can even make one wiser and more careful than people who did not go through such storms" (1920–1933, p. 242). Freud had arguably never experienced such storms or had never "worked through them". Their respective experiences of adolescence, specifically the theme of transgressive sexuality, were discussed in the context of a theoretical-clinical debate on the active technique.

In a letter of 1st May 1932, Ferenczi wrote that he had prepared himself for the reproaches addressed to him. Responding to Freud's criticism regarding his months of silence, he spoke about his isolation linked to his case work.

> Whatever the favoring motive of such isolation may be, it is not altogether anything bad or reprehensible; everyone probably has to go through such periods, which, with me, to be sure, turned up somewhat late, or, as you once wrote, as a belated puberty crisis.
>
> (Ibid., p. 431)

Yet Ferenczi did not have the same understanding of this crisis; while for Freud it was a kind of repeated sexual explosion, he saw it instead as a prolonged and belated adolescence. A deeper self-analysis revealed that since his early childhood, he tended to get into situations he could only master through an exceptionally large exertion of strength. "I never allowed myself a real psychic vacation", he wrote. He now wanted to take rest from this kind of super-performance lasting half a lifetime and immerse himself in a kind of scientific "Poetry and Truth" – a reference to both Freud and Goethe.

"But you should leave the island of dreams which you inhabit with your fantasy children" (Ibid., 433), Freud responded apropos Ferenczi's new involvement in the struggle. He criticised both his adolescent infantilism, which prevented Ferenczi from reaching the register of adult men, but also his supposed avoidance of this virile struggle. In this context, adolescence, daydreaming and femininity were all given a pejorative meaning.

Ferenczi responded (Ibid, p. 435) by speaking of his "dream-life", "daydreams" or again his "puberty crisis", taking the adolescent position as not necessarily pathological. What he argued for had to do more with grasping the elaborative potential of regression, even at the cost of certain regressive tendencies, which were not in themselves pathological. He defended a type of anticipated notion of the adolescent process, composed of back-and-forth movements between regression and working through. He added that "out of the relative confusion something useful will develop and has already developed" (Ibid.).

Being the president of the psychoanalytic movement was part of the process of growing up, but without recognising his belated puberty as a symptom. He initially accepted the candidacy, with the active support of Anna Freud and some others, but after a "long, anguished hesitation" he decided to renounce it (p. 441). He had gotten himself into a critical and self-critical stage in his work, which required him to make extensions and corrections to his practical and theoretical views. He therefore felt his position was not commensurate with the dignity of a president, "whose main concern should be conserving and consolidating what already exists" (Ibid.). It would have been dishonest to occupy this position at this time. This confirmed an impasse in the transmission between Freud and Ferenczi based on a traumatised filiation. Ferenczi seems to have been unable to identify with the maintaining of a tradition, whether clinically or institutionally. Occupying this paternal place would have meant having to drop his idealisation and make space for criticism. This came too late for him to be able to work through the central conflict: to enter the world of men, one must symbolically kill the father, even if one receives his endorsement.

Ferenczi indicated that he had no ambitions of founding a new school and stressed that his decision was led by a belief that Freud would not have wanted such a highly critical president. He was disappointed by his publications being considered as potentially harmful to the cause and hoped that Freud would let go of this idea. He concluded,

> I also have to concede that more courage and more open talk on my part about practical and theoretical things would have been advantageous to me. But, unfortunately, there is usually a lack of such courage in those who are younger and weaker.
>
> (p. 444)

4.3.8 Homosexuality, paranoia and de-sensualisation

In psychoanalytic literature, understanding the rapport between Freud and Ferenczi, no matter how subtle, has generally not made any references to the role played by adolescence, despite Freud's resounding "diagnosis" of third puberty at the peak of the crisis between them. This is nevertheless only one among the many elements related to adolescence present in their relationship. Over its course, we see that adolescence in fact permeated this connection, against the backdrop of a father-son conflict, in which a passionate and poorly sublimated homosexuality arguably mobilised a paranoiac position, due to the lack of a finer elaboration of the female position. At its centre was a pubertal Oedipus complex which was not worked through and instead created a conflict, between Ferenczi's demands for independence and Freud's defensive and excessively rigid, allegedly paternal position.

We find the effects of this negative transference in Ferenczi's "treatment" in both the active technique, which aimed to overcome the stagnation of repetition, and in the relaxation technique he introduced. Ferenczi wrote:

> My own analysis could not be pursued deep enough because my analyst (by his own admission, of a narcissistic nature), with his strong determination to be healthy and his antipathy towards any weaknesses or abnormalities, could not follow me down into these depths, and introduced the 'educational' stage too soon. Just as Freud's strength lies in firmness of education, so mine lies in the depth of the relaxation technique.
>
> (Ferenczi, 1995, p. 62)

Their dialogue brought into play two different images: first, that of Ferenczi's free and erratic genital sexuality – a demon, albeit a middle-aged one, in other words the same reproach Freud had already made to his teenage friend Eduard Silberstein; and second, the image of Freud as rigidly pedagogical, which we could see as an effort to preserve the link with his own father, based on the refusal (and the desire) of the female position. This brings us to a hypothesis that could well be applied to both men: both of them had in fact struggled with the necessary de-sensualisation of the father-son relationship during adolescence, which would have opened the way towards its potential conclusion. In Freud's case, these retroactive effects of his youth suggest that the manic euphoria of his apparent "triumph" over homosexuality, brought to a conflict in a paranoiac mode, was followed by a more depressive stage. The latter gave space to those parts of his adolescence that could not have been worked through and instead remained an active zone of conflict in his adult life.

Notes

1 Parts of this chapter have previously been published in *Les Lettres de Société de Psychanalyse Freudienne* in 2016.
2 At the time, the German terms *Adolescenz* and *Pubertät* were used interchangeably. On a closer look, we see that Freud most often uses the latter to speak about adolescence rather than about puberty in the strictly physiological sense of the term.

Chapter 5

The infantile as a screen against the pubertal

Our journey through Freud's adolescence has given us a sense not just of the traits of his personality and psychic conflicts, but also his bisexual openness, which lasted beyond adolescence, alongside an over-investment of psychic life, which was not just defensive. His interest in human truth, his need to believe (De Mijolla-Mellor, 2002) and rewrite his history into a family romance which itself was transformed into a theory, repeatedly reworked by his new insights, all contributed to his exceptional creativity. His long relationship with Eduard Silberstein represents a model of all relationships: a passionate idealisation, a need to find an "inseparable" object that evoked the idea of a twin-like bond, bisexuality, intellectualisation and angry ambivalence were present in this relationship and in many others later on. With Ferenczi, his favourite psychoanalyst "son", adolescence regularly emerged as a theme of their relationship, one that was rarely theorised but often active in their discussions, a line of flight which, even though named, largely escaped its protagonists. This line of flight in chiaroscuro was significant in terms of Freud's ambivalent relationship to adolescence, which he often perceived negatively but which remained a source of a nostalgia. Before we conclude, let us take a final look on what Freud's adolescence shows us in terms of his object relations.

5.1 Mother and sister

Our journey in Freudland has shown us other portraits, both realistic and fantasised, besides that of the young poet and researcher. Parental figures were at the forefront of this overall trend: the figure of the father, contrary to that of the mother, was very present both during adolescence and in its aftermath, namely in Freud's work on dreams. The often kindly presence of his father as well as the ambivalent conflicts with his various substitutes suggest a gap between the "real" father and the one Freud imagined. Did he take on part of the ambivalence felt towards his mother, as Abraham (1982) has suggested? This is a reasonable hypothesis, given young's Freud's raging murderous and homosexual conflicts, which were often very passionate. It is true that Freud had a conquering spirit, but he was also hurt by the many disappointments and disillusionments he encountered while struggling for recognition from his favourite great men. His search for identification through

DOI: 10.4324/9781003437062-6

recognition was part of a double tendency: an Oedipal desire for a tender but weakened father and, related to this, a lack of a firmer or even authoritarian figure, which fuelled his sense of lacking support and acted as an element of ambivalence in his relationship to the paternal imago.

As to the factors that contributed to his choice of profession, I would argue that psychoanalysis offered a more seductive perspective than that of a writer, even though ultimately Freud joined the two professions together. Driven by a fantasy of self-engendering linked to the megalomaniac desire of becoming a great man, Freud pursued his adolescent fantasy all the way to the end, exploring a *terra incognita* where no one could overshadow him. Emerging from the shadow of his father, as well as from those of his teachers and the knowledge they had transmitted to him, was key to his emancipation as a man.

In his descriptions of his childhood, the mother is much less present than the father, but in fact occupied an equally central place in the movements and transferences of his adolescent life. We see this in the double image of the witch (*The Dialogue of the Dogs*, the mother of the girl seduced by Eduard) and the idealised woman-child (the angel from the train, Gisela's mother). Note that in this condensed version, the mother-daughter duo has a rather straightforward interpretation: the angel, as a form of over-valuing of women, marks a defensive desexualisation of the incestuous object. Freud's fascination with these mother-daughter duos reminds us of his own family constellation: the four sisters who followed his birth before the arrival of his younger brother. As a young child, Freud was repeatedly confronted by a mother occupied with these baby girls, so that we may wonder if, in order to gain access to her, he was not forced to make an association between mother and daughter. This also reminds us of his relationship with his oldest sister Anna, which was conflict-ridden and rivalrous to say the least. Like a screen memory, the adolescent fascination tinged with idealisation would then mask and cover over the rivalrous hate towards his sister. Still, we could argue that a trace of this fascination was rather persistent in his theory. In 1912, he wrote that

> it sounds not only disagreeable but also paradoxical, yet it must nevertheless be said that anyone who is to be really free and happy in love must have surmounted his respect for women and have come to terms with the idea of incest with his mother or[1] sister.
>
> (Freud, 1912, p. 186)

Interestingly, while the Oedipus complex usually relies on a triangular model – mother-father-child – in this text, which is part of Freud's *Contributions to the Psychology of Love*, which largely deals with adolescence, we instead see a quadrangle, unless it is another form of triangulation, where a sister takes the father's place.

Adolescence brings certain archaic maternal images to the surface, as attested to by the image of women as the source of danger, which appear in Freud's dream associations around the tale of Mélusine. Although in Freud's writing his memories and associations with his mother are rather discreet, we are still left with multiple representations of the maternal figure that help us grasp what I have described as a phobic attitude towards girls in Freud's adolescence. Because of his repeated reliance on the psychic life of young people, Freud (1910b, 1912, 1918) largely exploited these different male figurations of femininity.

5.2   A youth in hiding

Looking at the way Freud treated his own adolescence, we might at first think that it was more strongly repressed than his childhood. However, on reading his letters to Martha (Freud, 1873–1939) as well as certain theoretical passages, we come to a different conclusion, which is nevertheless compatible with the first. On looking back, Freud saw his adolescent conflicts as less unbearable, their memories and reconstructions less bitter. For a teenage boy, the fantasies experienced as potentially perverse were a source of anxiety for several reasons: they seemed abnormal both personally and socially, there was a fear of having criminal desires, of being bad, a fear of being rejected, as well as a sense of extreme solitude, due to the sense of being the only one to have these kinds of fantasies and the only one responsible for them. Fundamentally, the fear that condensed these deep-seated and varied anxieties was the fear of going mad, like the monk with incestuous fantasies in the first book that had so impressed Freud as a teenager.

Another more relative aspect is that Freud seems to open up more easily about his rivalries, conflicts and desire for revenge, while remaining more discreet about his teenage sexual fantasies, more prone to censorship. What might seem natural when one exposes oneself the way Freud does, is not simply explained but, as we have seen, subject to a great many rationalisations, which eventually draw our attention: why so many justifications rather than a simple exposition which the reader could easily understand? When he describes certain episodes from his childhood, for example urinating in his parents' bedroom and being caught by his father, who says the child will come to nothing, i.e., a supposedly major narcissistic wound in Freud's life, he expresses no hesitations as to presenting this material. But is there a comparable equivalent regarding his teenage sexuality? The stories of adolescence are more subdued, as if covered by a veil of respectability, confirming the impression that the infantile may sometimes act as a screen against the pubertal, while the latter mobilises the deep and hidden fantasies of infantile sexual life. The distortion of the story of Gisela (Freud, 1899) is a key example of this overall tendency. It is also confirmed by Freud's comments on his passion for reading, in the context of the dream of the botanical monograph. The dream initially brings up an infantile memory, before Freud realises that this memory in fact covers over his teenage bibliophilia.

As a result, we can infer that this covering over of adolescence by the infantile acted as an impediment to further theorisation of adolescence in Freud's work. It is clear that Freud wanted to avoid the risk of infantile sexuality being put on par or even conflated with post-pubertal sexuality, which in the common sense was too closely related to the so-called adult sexuality.

5.3   Biographical-theoretical perspectives

We should add that while Freud's self-analysis allowed him to recover his memories of adolescence, this work of remembering seems to have come to an end in its last theorisation, namely in the chapter on the transformations of puberty included in the other major work of this crucial period (Freud, 1905a). At first, we might think that there was no real follow-up to this that would concern adolescence directly; however, some of the essential works on metapsychology could be said to carry clear traces of Freud's adolescence. We have already identified how closely his biography and theory were entangled in the paper on screen memories and the two texts on the *Uncanny* and the *Disturbance of Memory on the Acropolis*, to which we added his letter to Schnitzler. This thematic pole also includes the subjects of neurasthenia, the actual neuroses, the anxiety neurosis (Freud, 1895, 1898), masturbation, a large part of his theory of hysteria and of bisexuality as its corollary – all of these at a critical moment in the birth of psychoanalysis. The latter was also marked by the discovery of retroaction (*après-coup*) in the case of Emma, based on her memories of adolescence and on Freud's own recollections in the case of screen memories (1950 [1895], 1899). Anzieu (1989) sees Emma's image, after her botched nose surgery, as a bleeding virgin sacrificed on the altar of the homosexual connection between Fliess and Freud (Houssier, 2018a). The psychoanalytic theory emerging from various clinical situations, from discussions with Fliess and Freud's analysis of his own dreams (Freud, 1900) largely revolved around cases of young people. It was a form of co-creation in the sense that Freud constructed his hypotheses at a time where he was again experiencing a passionate friendship with a new double. Fliess followed after Silberstein; for several idyllic years, Freud maintained the secret hope of "merging" their respective theories (Vermorel, 2018, p. 60).

We could also mention *Contributions to the Psychology of Love* or Freud's phylogenetic theory and its murderous gang of young men (Freud, 1910–1918). In this interval, we can also situate the naming of the Oedipus complex which Abraham identified as a chance encounter between a young man and his father. This project of rereading Freud's theoretical foundations based on his experience of adolescence is still to be undertaken. It might bring us a new understanding of him personally and of some of the key aspects of his theory, without forgetting the effects of his theorisation as based on many clinical cases, not only of Dora and the young female homosexual. Today, these "young people", as Freud described them, can be given their rightful place as adolescents in Freud's theory. Many other examples such as *A Child Is Being Beaten* (Freud, 1919b) or *The Rat Man* case (1909) point to the continued relevance of the question of adolescence in his theory, as well as its author's ambivalent relationship to this subject. Freud was probably too attached to the infantile to understand the importance of the scenes from puberty, despite the typical fantasies that may have shown him the way. Therefore, the working through undertaken in the *Three Essays* gradually faded away, without ever really disappearing from his theory, consciously or not. Despite the nostalgia provoked by a request for Freud to write a few memories of his school days (Freud, 1914), adolescence as a theoretical topic seemed more or less abandoned – unless we consider this was not in fact the case. The myth of origins is a paradigmatic example of this thematic distancing, a de-centred theoretical continuity (Houssier, 2013). The myth – killing one's father to internalise what he symbolically represents, thus opening the door to sexual and social life – echoes today as an essential part of the dynamics of adolescence. Freud (1933) outlined this paradigm by positing a primordial moment, an actual castration carried out by a father jealous of his teenage sons.

5.4   Struggling against the adolescence in oneself

Once contextualised, Freud's adolescence can be seen as paradigmatic of adolescence in general, including its massive repression, a refusal to return to its overly intense affects, similarly to infantile amnesia. Freud's self-analysis enabled him to return to certain aspects of his adolescence, perhaps to discover the importance of retroaction that connected the infantile to the pubertal, as suggested in his letter to Rolland (Freud, 1936). The most virulent and regressive parts of the adolescent process and the transformations it brought were probably avoided or transformed as if through dream-work. However, adolescence continued to operate in him, as shown by the *a posteriori* connections between his present life, memories and his theoretical work. Because he regularly drew on the psychic lives of his young patients (Houssier, Christaki, 2016), whom we would today consider adolescents, Freud largely exploited their different representation of femininity as the dark continent in man's psychic life. Another possible hypothesis arises when trying to understand why, given the frequency of young people coming to analysis, adolescence remained under-theorised, with the exception of the third essay on the theory of sexuality, and despite Freud's argument that it constituted the fourth and last stage of human sexuality.

A number of things suggest this was a defensive move. Freud did not want to create a confusion between infantile and post-pubertal sexuality, thus protecting his fundamental discovery. If we agree with him that at times, such as in the case of his adolescent passion for books, the infantile served as a screen against adolescent memories, we may wonder if his scientific discovery was not in fact underpinned by a repression of adolescence in favour of the infantile. The screen memory would therefore have another function: namely as a defence against adolescent fantasies that amplified those of the child, no longer protected by his innocence. The loss of innocence is indeed one of the most significant differences between the child and the adolescent – what may be ordinary or even amusing in an unsuspicious child becomes vulgar and violent in the psychic life of a teenager. The vocabulary used by Freud regularly shows traces of this split: infantile innocence is juxtaposed against the (sexual) transgression of adolescence.

The pan-sexualism of which Freud was often accused was therefore linked to the way in which the infantile served as a screen against the pubertal, as a defence against adolescence and its bitter, sad and traumatic memories. Freud was right to sexualise childhood, but he stayed away from theorising adolescence. We find this distancing also in the clinical field, when he would diagnose neurosis in adolescents just thirteen years old (Freud, 1900). This confusion between hysteria and adolescence, which went hand in hand with a denial of adolescence in his young patient, is most marked in the case of Dora (Freud, 1905b). The contemporary scientific context with respect to the treatment of hysteria, which included hypnosis, as well as the rivalry between Freud and Pierre Janet with regards to neurosis and its aetiology, played a key role in this reductive clinical position. His biographical-created theory (Houssier, 2018c) was therefore a constant source of reflections, fuelling both the theory and the practice of psychoanalysis.

5.5   A new mystery in Freud's country

The systematic revision of Freud's clinical work with young people, which was so valuable to him, as well as an exploration of the influence of adolescence on his theory should complete this biographical diptych, in which these two perspectives are already present. We are nevertheless still faced with an enigma: Freud constructed psychoanalytic theory based on two foundational myths, the Oedipus and the primal horde, i.e., two stories of young men driven by a desire to murder their father. However, while Freud did attend to adolescence both clinically and theoretically, after 1906 he made no more attempts to deepen its theorisation. The hypothesis that emerges is therefore that his adolescence was indeed subject to repression, but it remained alive in Freud's psyche as an unsettling current, associated with a series of negative fantasies.

This hypothesis has its underside: in a more idealised manner, Jones (1958) highlighted Freud's youthful enthusiasm at the beginning of the First World War by linking it to his interest in the war of 1870, when he was fifteen years old. Subsequently, when Vermorel (2018) discussed the construction of Freud's personal novel, he founded it on the fantasy of a solitary hero, alone against all odds. This idea is well known, but it is rarely or indeed never connected to the typical fantasies of adolescence, the fantasy of the seductive Oedipal hero, alone against his father, whom he must kill again and again. This gesture attests to a bisexual identification undermined by the contiguity between an idealisation of the father and his murder, a duality subsequently displaced onto the band of brothers, the sons of the primal horde represented by Freud's disciples.

His self-analysis, which began during adolescence and was pursued throughout his life, could be seen as an extension of his teenage diary, associated with the need for a double to escape the agony of solitude. Did Freud remain stuck in an adolescent position, attached to the myth of the hero, throughout his life? If creation was a way of fending off death, Freud had arguably maintained a constant investment of this personal myth since his teenage years, relying on his exceptional creative abilities, and hence remained too fixated in this position to be able to work through it beyond the third essay on the theory of sexuality. What creative work and adolescence have in common is a certain destabilisation of the ego's boundaries (Houssier et al., 2017), which at times can go as far as depersonalisation. This highly particular feeling, the importance of which throughout Freud's biography I have previously highlighted (Houssier, 2018a), illustrates precisely the archaic maternal feminine which remained in tension for Freud.

As Vermorel suggests (2018), in some of his relationships, for example with Rolland, Freud may have found a transferential symbiosis as his mother's favourite child. This departure point was gradually transformed into the narcissistic image of a hero above others, whose grandiose project was to create an immortal body of work. Creativity, fuelled by an adolescent fantasy of self-engendering, drove him to explore the foundations of unconscious psychic life. To fight against this kind of regression, what better way but to invent a detour, relying on the paternal figure, both in life and in work? Vermorel's perspective is therefore that Freud was an incestuous hero, the favourite child of his mother, who protected him from the violence of the father of the primal horde, killed with his mother's blessing. We could add that Freud's fascination with the myth of the primal horde, with a story of origins, concurs with his fantasy of self-engendering. The myth of the horde was part of a process of self-historicisation which in fact stemmed from the self-creation of adolescence.

Rather than femininity or primal homosexuality, themes where Freud always maintained a certain self-analytical lucidity, adolescence would then be the true dark continent, one that, given its lack of theorisation, regularly returned to haunt Freud's object relations. Just to give another example: when Freud wrote to Emma Eckstein some years after her psychoanalytic treatment, he returned to the theme of the double and femininity. "All these events . . . again filled me with respect for the primordial femininity against which I am constantly fighting" (Masson, 1984, p. 219). Yet the limits of his self-analysis did not concern so much his fight against femininity, but rather the question of adolescence, both his own and that of his patients. We should finally keep in mind that the need to integrate one's femininity, which continued to represent a struggle for Freud, is very much part of the adolescent process.

It nevertheless remains the case that at the closing of this biographical diptych, new areas of research appear in the intermediary space between Freud's life and his work. And so, new frontiers emerge in Freud's world – let's rise to the challenge!

Note

1 The use of "or" seems inclusive here.

Bibliography

Abraham, K. (1922). Rescue and murder of the father in neurotic phantasies. *International Journal of Psychoanalysis*, 3: 467–474.

Abraham, R. (1982). Freud's mother and the formulation of the oedipal father. *The Psychoanalytic Review*, 69: 441–453.

Anzieu, D. (1989). *L'auto-analyse de Freud*. Paris: PUF.

Barande, I. (1972). *Sándor Ferenczi*. Paris: Payot.

Bernfeld, S. (1944). Freud's earliest theories and the school of Helmholtz. *Psychoanalytic Quarterly*, 13: 341–362.

Bernfeld, S. (1951). Sigmund Freud, M. D., 1882–1885. *International Journal of the Psychoanalysis*, 32: 204–217.

Bernfeld, S. (1953). Freud's studies on cocaine. In: R. Byck (Ed.), *Cocaine Papers Sigmund Freud*. New York: Stonehill, 1975, pp. 323–352.

Blum, H. (2001). Freud's private mini-monograph on his own dreams. A contribution to the celebration of the centenary of the interpretation of dreams. *The International Journal of Psychoanalysis*, 82 (5): 953–964.

Boehlich, W. (1900). Introduction. In: S. Freud (Ed.), *Lettres de jeunesse*. Paris: Gallimard, 1990, pp. 17–31.

Breger, L. (2000). *Freud: Darkness in the Midst of Vision*. New York: Wiley.

Busch, W. (1865). *Max et Moritz. Pierre l'Ébouriffé et consorts*. Genève: Éditions La joie de lire, 2005, pp. 167–191.

De Mijolla, A. (Ed.) (2002). *Dictionnaire international de la psychanalyse*. Paris: Calmann-Lévy.

De Mijolla-Mellor, S. (2002). *Le besoin de savoir: théories et mythes magico-sexuels dans l'enfance*. Paris: Dunod.

Eissler, K. R. (1955). *Compte-rendu d'une lettre de Marie Paneth (belle-fille de Joseph Paneth)*. Sigmund Freud Archives, Washington Library, 7th March 1955.

Eissler, K. R. (1978). Creativity and adolescence: The effect of trauma in Freud's adolescence. *The Psychoanalytic Study of the Child*, 33: 461–518.

Eissler, K. R. (2006). Esquisse biographique. In: K. Eissler, E. Freud, L. Freud, I. Grubrich Simitis, W. Fleckhaus (Eds.), *Sigmund Freud. Lieux, visages, objets*. Paris: Gallimard, pp. 10–38.

Erikson, E. (1950). *Childhood and Society*. London: W.W. Norton & Company.

Fabre, N. (2014). Étrange double, double étranger. *Imaginaire & Inconscient*, 14 (2): 15–22.

Ferenczi, S. (1921–1933). *The Ferenczi-Groddeck Correspondence*. London: Open Gate Press, 2002.

Ferenczi, S. (1995). *The Clinical Diary of Sandor Ferenczi*. Edited by Judith Dupont. Cambridge, MA: Harvard University Press.

Freud, A. (1919). *Letter to Ernst Freud, 2 February 1919*. Freud Museum, London. Unpublished.

Freud, E. L. (1970). *The Letters of Sigmund Freud and Arnold Zweig*. New York: The International Psycho-Analytical Library, 84, pp. 1–184.

Freud, S. (1871–1881). *The Letters of Sigmund Freud to Eduard Silberstein, 1871–1881*. Edited by Walter Boehlich. Cambridge, MA: Harvard University Press, 1990.

Freud, S. (1873–1939). *Letters of Sigmund Freud (1873–1939)*. London: Hogarth Press, 1970.

Freud, S. (1877). Observation de la conformation de l'organe lobé de l'anguille décrit comme glande germinale mâle. In: P. Fédida, D. Widlöcher (Eds.), *Les évolutions phylogénétiques de l'individuation*. Paris: PUF, 1994, pp. 9–20.

Freud, S. (1887–1904). *The Complete Letters of Sigmund Freud to Wilhelm Fliess, 1887–1904*. Edited by M. Masson. Cambridge, MA: Harvard University Press, 1986.

Freud, S. (1895). On the grounds for detaching a particular syndrome from neurasthenia under the description 'Anxiety Neurosis'. *SE*, 3: 85–115. London: Hogarth Press.

Freud, S. (1898). Sexuality in the Aetiology of the neuroses. *SE*, 3: 259–285. London: Hogarth Press.

Freud, S. (1899). Screen memories. *SE*, 3: 299–322. London: Hogarth Press.

Freud, S. (1900). The interpretation of dreams. *SE*, 4: ix–627. London: Hogarth Press.

Freud, S. (1901a). On dreams. *SE*, 5: 629–686. London: Hogarth Press.

Freud, S. (1901b). The psychopathology of everyday life: Forgetting, slips of the tongue, bungled actions, superstitions and errors. *SE*, 6: vii–296. London: Hogarth Press.

Freud, S. (1905a). Three essays on the theory of sexuality. *SE*, 7: 123–246. London: Hogarth Press.

Freud, S. (1905b). Fragment of an analysis of a case of hysteria. *SE*, 7: 1–122. London: Hogarth Press.

Freud, S. (1908), in Nunberg H., Federn E. (dir.), Les Premiers Psychanalystes. Minutes de la Société psychanalytique de Vienne, 1908–1910, T. II, Paris, Gallimard, 1978.

Freud, S. (1909). Notes upon a case of obsessional neurosis. *SE*, 10: 151–318. London: Hogarth Press.

Freud, S. (1910a). Five lectures on psycho-analysis. *SE*, 11: 1–56. London: Hogarth Press.

Freud, S. (1910b). A special type of choice of object made by men (Contributions to the Psychology of Love I). *SE*, 11: 163–176.

Freud, S. (1910–1918). Contributions à la psychologie de la vie amoureuse. In: *La vie sexuelle*. Paris: PUF, 1969, pp. 47–80.

Freud, S. (1912). On the universal tendency to debasement in the sphere of love (Contributions to the Psychology of Love II). *SE*, 11: 177–190.

Freud, S. (1913 [1912–13]). Totem and taboo: Some points of agreement between the mental lives of savages and neurotics. *SE*, 13: vii–162. London: Hogarth Press.

Freud, S. (1914). Some reflections on schoolboy psychology. *SE*, 13: 239–244. London: Hogarth Press.

Freud, S. (1918). The taboo of virginity (Contributions to the Psychology of Love III). *SE*, 11: 191–208. London: Hogarth Press.

Freud, S. (1919a). The 'Uncanny'. *SE*, 17: 217–256. London: Hogarth Press.

Freud, S. (1919b). 'A Child Is Being Beaten': A contribution to the study of the origin of sexual perversions. *SE*, 17: 175–204. London: Hogarth Press.

Freud, S. (1920). The psychogenesis of a case of homosexuality in a woman. *SE*, 18: 145–172. London: Hogarth Press.

Freud, S. (1925). An autobiographical study. *SE*, 20: 1–74 London: Hogarth Press.

Freud, S. (1932). My contact with Josef Popper-Lynkeus. *SE*, 22: 217–224. London: Hogarth Press.

Freud, S. (1933). New introductory lectures on psycho-analysis. *SE*, 22: 1–182. London: Hogarth Press.

Freud, S. (1936). A disturbance of memory on the acropolis. *SE*, 22: 237–248. London: Hogarth Press.

Freud, S. (1937). L'analyse avec fin et l'analyse sans fin. In: *Résultats, Idées, Problèmes, T. 2*. Paris: PUF, 1985, pp. 231–268.

Freud, S. (1950 [1895]). Project for a scientific psychology. *SE*, 1: 281–391

Freud, S., Ferenczi, S. (1908–1914). *The Correspondence of Sigmund Freud and Sándor Ferenczi*, Volume 1. Cambridge, MA: Harvard University Press, 1993.

Freud, S., Ferenczi, S. (1914–1919). *The Correspondence of Sigmund Freud and Sándor Ferenczi*, Volume 2. Cambridge, MA: Harvard University Press, 1996.

Freud, S., Ferenczi, S. (1920–1933). *The Correspondence of Sigmund Freud and Sándor Ferenczi*, Volume 3. Cambridge, MA: Harvard University Press, 2000.

Gallo, R. (2009). Freud's Spanish: Bilingualism and bisexuality. *Psychoanalysis and History*, 11: 5–40.

Grubrich-Simitis, I., Lortholary, B. (2012). L'affectif et la théorie Sigmund et Martha: prélude Freudien. Germes de concepts psychanalytiques fondamentaux. À propos des lettres de fiancés de Sigmund Freud et Martha Bernays. *Revue Française de Psychanalyse*, 3 (76): 779–795.

Hamilton, J. W. (2002). Freud and the suicide of Pauline Silberstein. *Psychoanalytic Review*, 89: 889–909.

Hardin, H. T. (1987). On the vicissitudes of Freud's early mothering: I. Early environment and loss. *Psychoanalytic Quarterly*, 56: 628–644.

Houssier, F. (2010). *Anna Freud et son école. Créativité et controverses*. Paris: Campagne-Première.

Houssier, F. (2013). *Meurtres dans la famille*. Paris: Dunod.

Houssier, F. (2015a). Freud adolescent. In: R. Perron, S. Missonnier (Eds.), *Freud. Les Cahiers de l'Herne*. Paris: Editions de L'Herne, pp. 31–37.

Houssier, F. (2015b). L'adolescence de Freud dans "L'interprétation du rêve". *Les lettres de la SPF*, 33: 123–138.

Houssier, F. (2016). Entre S. Freud et S. Ferenczi, un Oedipe pubertaire? *Les lettres de la SPF*, 35: 157–173.

Houssier, F. (2017a). S. Freud et ses sorcières: représentations archaïques de la figure maternelle à l'adolescence. *Le Divan Familial*, 39: 205–215.

Houssier, F. (2017b). Freud adolescent ou les langages du corps: nager, marcher, grimper. In: F. Houssier (Ed.), *Le sport à l'adolescence. Entre violence et sublimation*. Paris, In Press, pp. 23–44.

Houssier, F. (2018a). *Freud Adolescent*. Paris: Campagne-Première.

Houssier, F. (2018b). Boulimie et délinquance: féminin incestuel dans le mouvement de personnalisation-différenciation, *Adolescence*, 36 (1): 85–96.

Houssier, F. (Ed.) (2018c). *S. Freud et ses transferts*. Paris, In Press.

Houssier, F. et al. (Eds.) (2018). *Cartes postales, notes et lettres. De Sigmund Freud à Paul Federn (1905–1938)*. Paris: Ithaque.

Houssier, F., Bonnichon, D., Vlachopoulou, X., Blanc, A. (2017). Paul Federn, la psychanalyse à ses frontières. In: *Paul Federn. Investissement du moi et actes manqués*. Paris: Ithaque, pp. 9–32.

Houssier, F., Chagnon, J.-Y. (2016). Accompagner son fils adolescent: Freud entre père et fils, *Cliopsy (Revue Psycinfo en Sciences de l'éducation)*, 16: 9–23.

Houssier, F., Christaki, A. (2016). Folie pubertaire et sexualité diabolique dans les débuts de la psychanalyse. *Topique*, 134: 157–170.

Houssier, F., Gutton, P. (2018). Sigmund Freud, un adolescent (pas) comme les autres. *Adolescence*, 36 (2): 401–418.

Jones, E. (1954). *Sigmund Freud, Life and Death, Volume One: The Young Freud, 1856–1900.* London: Hogarth Press.

Jones, E. (1958). *Sigmund Freud, Life and Death, Volume Two: Years of Maturity, 1901–1919.* London: Hogarth Press.

Kanzer, M. (1976). Freud and his literary doubles. *American Imago*, 33: 231–243.

Lotto, D. (2001). Freud's struggle with misogyny: Homosexuality and guilt in the dream of Irma's injection. *Journal of the American Psychoanalytic Association*, 49: 1289–1313.

Masson, J. M. (1984). *Le reel escamoté.* Paris: Aubier.

Nunberg, H., Federn, E. (Eds.) (1967). *Minutes of the Vienna Psychoanalytic Society, 1908–1910*, Volume 2. Madison, CT: International Universities Press.

Papini, G. (1973). A visit to Freud (May 8 1934). In: H. M. Ruytenbeck (Ed.), *Freud as We Know Him*. Detroit: Wayne State University Press, pp. 98–102.

Prado de Oliveira, L. E. (2011). *Sándor Ferenczi, la psychanalyse autrement.* Paris: A. Colin.

Roudinesco, E. (2016). *Freud: In His Time and Ours.* Cambridge, MA: Harvard University Press.

Roussillon, R., Golse, B. (2010). *La naissance de l'objet.* Paris: PUF.

Sabourin, P. (2011). *Sándor Ferenczi, un pionnier de la clinique.* Paris: Campagne-Première.

Schavelzon, J. (1983). *Freud, un paciente con cancer.* Buenos Aires: Paidos.

Shur, M. (1972a). *Freud: Living and Dying.* New York: International Universities Press.

Shur, M. (1972b). *La mort dans la vie de Freud.* Paris: Gallimard.

Trosman, H. (1969). The cryptomnesic fragment in the discovery of free association. *The Journal of the American Psychoanalytic Association*, 17: 489–510.

Trosman, H. (1973). Freud's cultural background. *The Annual of Psychoanalysis*, 1: 318–335.

Vermorel, H. S. (2018). *Freud et R. Rolland. Un dialogue.* Paris: Albin Michel.

Wittels, F. (1924). *Freud et la femme-enfant.* Paris: PUF, 1999.

Index

For Product Safety Concerns and Information please contact our EU
representative GPSR@taylorandfrancis.com
Taylor & Francis Verlag GmbH, Kaufingerstraße 24, 80331 München, Germany